THUMBS UP

' "The Zebra" and I were topping the bill at Southampton Town Hall, and as I walked to the ring I saw the most beautiful girl sitting in the centre of the hall, about four seats in from the aisle. I thought, what a smasher! I must have a talk with her. The Zebra fought dirty as usual and the crowd got mad at him. So in the third round I contrived to get the Zebra's hand on my face and I screamed and fell out of the ring yelling "I'm blinded, I'm blinded." I staggered and zig-zagged down the aisle, trying to get to the girl. The hardest thing was getting past the sympathetic punters who wanted to help me! Half way through the hall, four seats in, I laid my head on her lap. She didn't know what was happening. I cuddled up and told her she was smashing and asked her to come to my dressing room after the fight. Then the customers were onto me and pulling me to the ring to go and kill the Zebra. We put on a fantastic display; but I'm sorry to say the girl didn't turn up.'

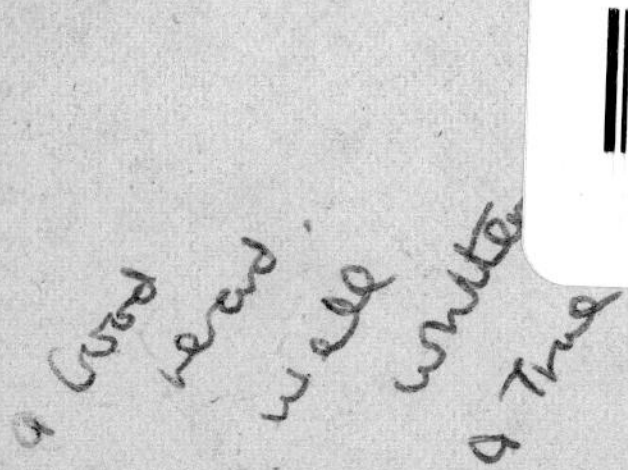

THUMBS UP

An autobiography
by
Joe Cornelius

A STAR BOOK
published by
the Paperback Division of
W. H. ALLEN & CO. PLC

A Star Book
Published in 1984
by the Paperback Division of
W. H. Allen & Co. PLC
44 Hill Street, London W1X 8LB

Printed and bound in Great Britain by
Cox & Wyman Ltd, Reading

ISBN 0 352 315199

Contents

To Lindi,
who made me find love

An Explanation

To feel that all your life
you've been so lonely
although there are and were
a thousand people all around
and now, at last to know how love feels.
I'm not thinking about the body feelings,
the feelings in the groin.
I'm talking about the feelings in the heart,
the head
and in something
I'm not even sure just where it is.
It's just a something deep inside
making you sad, happy and wanting
to break your fucking heart.
I'm sure some of you know what I mean,
it's a feeling all on its own
that brings down giants to mere whimpering babies
helpless to do a thing about it.
If only you could see it, fight it,
kick the living shit out of it and stop the pain.
And yet you're pleased to suffer,
at least you're feeling
and you know the pain is just the other side of love
and that it can be beautiful, wholesome, pure
like nothing in this world.
This terrible, wonderful feeling,
you know what love is . . . it's murder.

1

Best Way Out

In my twenty years in the wrestling game I had more than three and a half thousand fights – but never a better finish than when I fought Ferenc Gida. It was in 1956, in Belgium where I was already a big name. I was billed as Cor Argentino from Portugal. I got that name because when I first went out there they needed more international colour and, being a newcomer, I was the colour. In those early days it didn't matter to me what they called me so long as I got a fight. I was hungry to learn and get to the top.

But now I was a star and there were only two names on the posters that night in Antwerp: Cor Argentino and Ferenc Gida from Hungary. Gida was a great wrestler, and a great gentleman – and there aren't many of those in the business, I can tell you. He was one of the men who helped this cockney kid on his way up. It was an honour to be fighting him.

The Belgians love their wrestling, and the town was bubbling with excitement. This was something different: two giants of the ring – Gida, the dignified and much-loved master of the art, and myself, the young clown who was also a pretty good wrestler. The arena was packed with four thousand people and the atmosphere was tense. The crowd sensed that something sensational was going to happen. And it did.

Gida, seventeen-and-a-half stone and in his mid-thirties, entered first with his slow, long Hungarian strides, proud and confident, with the crowd cheering like mad. He was already in the ring when I appeared; fifteen stone and in my mid-twenties, my gold lamé cloak shimmering under the lights and my thick black hair beautifully groomed: smiling, waving and throwing kisses, letting the crowd know I loved them as much as they loved me. They knew I was going to give them a good time and enjoy myself whatever happened.

As we went to our corners the crowd hushed. They didn't want to miss anything, not even our instructions from the referee. Normally I would be clowning and messing about in my corner but this night I was deadly serious, and the crowd knew that Cor Argentino meant business.

We came out of our corners, came together like two bulls in the referee's hold, broke, came together again in a clash and broke – but as we broke Gida boomeranged me. He took both my legs up around my thighs, one either side of him, fell back with his knees in the small of my back – and heaved. It was one of his specialities. I sailed through the air and got tangled up with the ropes. The crowd gasped and stood as one.

I thought, 'Blimey, that was good. I bet if I tried I

could really fly out of the ring.' So, as Gida came in again, I said, 'Encore.' He took my legs and back he went, but this time I was helping. I tensed my body and as he heaved so did I. I flew – and how I flew! I went over the top of the ropes and wasn't losing any height. I thought, 'Christ, where am I going?' I landed about five rows back on the wooden floor of the aisle. Wow! What a throw! The crowd were going mad, climbing over each other trying to see what had happened. But I was fine. I hadn't felt a thing, which in itself was a miracle, considering I had travelled about twenty feet from ten feet up and crashed onto the floor! Then the showman in me took over. I thought, 'There can never be a finish like this again!' and I decided to lie there quite still. They didn't even count me out, they probably thought I was dead. The hall was silent as the referee and seconds crowded round me. Relieved to find me alive, but assuming I was badly damaged, Lovely Jan, the referee, a big strong man, lifted me gently onto his shoulder to carry me to the dressing rooms which were quite a long way from the ring.

As we went down the aisle I had my hand down his trousers and put my thumb up his arse. Was he surprised! He was walking like a poof and the sweat was breaking out all over him. Poor Jan was wishing he had left me on the floor. When eventually we got to the dressing rooms he dropped me and collapsed on a chair calling me all the bastards under the sun. Then the promoter came rushing in.

'Cor, Cor, are you okay?' he asked.

'Yes,' I said, 'I'm fine – but what a finish!'

He stopped in his tracks, paused and said, 'Yes, but so soon?'

I explained that there could never be another finish like that and how it would make for a fabulous return match. He agreed and felt better, knowing the return bout would pack the biggest arena he could find. He went out to the crowd, told them I was all right and said he would put on a return fight at my instructions.

Gida met me later and called me a madman for taking such a chance, going out of the ring like that.

And now you know about my greatest finish, I'd better tell you how it all began – and how I came to be known as the 'Thumbs Up boy'.

2

From Here To Maturity

Dad never bought toys as such for us kids. He bought boxing gloves, chest expanders and punch balls. So it was no wonder my youngest brother Bill and I grew up loving sport. When he was eleven years old Bill weighed fourteen stone. Peter, the middle brother, and I were lightweights then but we were very strong. Dad put it all down to early morning chocolate and cakes. He was a printer working in Fleet Street, coming home at five in the morning and always waking us up with bars of chocolate and cakes which he'd bought at the all-night café. We'd polish them off and go back to sleep for an hour.

Apart from those feasts, we were brought up pretty strictly. We lived in Boyson Road, SE17, and we were real London kids. Our playground was among the stalls and barrows of the small market in Westmoreland Road.

As soon as I could toddle I'd be off out of the house and exploring the world outside. I was often found asleep on the pavement. By the time I was nearly three I wanted to climb everything in sight. One day I even climbed the kitchen dresser and upset pepper all over my face. The chemist down the road had to wash it out of my eyes; but that still didn't stop me climbing.

When we went to school in the Albany Road, Mum sent us off every day with clean shirts and socks. We'd leave the house looking like Little Lord Fauntleroys, and come back looking right little urchins.

Mum and Dad insisted on good manners and respect for elders. We were seen and not heard. But we were given plenty of love and trust. My brothers were both ginger-haired, but I was so dark my uncles called me Treacle. It was my touch of the tar brush I suppose. My great grandmother was Spanish and my great grandfather was an Army physical training instructor.

I didn't learn much at my first school. I got a bad headache every time there was a spelling lesson and the only subject I enjoyed was maths. (I still can't spell – and I'm not even all that good at adding up when I'm behind the bar.) But we had a democratic vote for School Captain, and I won. A friend of mine was the teacher's choice because he was brainy, but the boys voted for me because I was the best sportsman. I made all my mates stair monitors and prefects and we ran that school with discipline and respect. I shall never forget the morning we were all playing football in the playground when I spotted the headmistress coming through the school gates. I whistled like mad and made everybody stop playing and stand still until she had walked the length of the playground and into the school, nodding to me as she passed. Later, in the main hall, she congratulated me and all the boys for being such gentlemen. I was only eleven, but I was so proud at that moment. You know, looking back it hardly seems possible that we were all so young.

While I was at the Albany Road School, Mum decided to send Peter and me to tap-dancing lessons. Peter didn't take to it but I was a natural, so good that the teacher offered me free lessons. But our Mum insisted on paying.

One day she sent me off to the lesson with a ten-shilling note because she hadn't got any loose change. It was the last bit of money in her purse. When I got back, Mum wanted a coin for the gas meter and asked me for her change. 'Oh Mum,' I said, 'I found some money in my pocket on the way home and forgot it was yours so I treated all my pals to pie and mash.' With that, my five-foot-nothing Mum threw me to the ground and holding onto the kitchen table stamped all over me. It was my first wrestling lesson.

My school reports at that time described me as 'a little gentleman'. And I must have been because I took a lot of bullying from a Greek boy named Darkie who lived opposite us, without ever fighting back. Until the day Mum told me to give him a thrashing and I whacked him so hard his mother came round and kicked up hell with mine. But our Mum won that bout too, and we never had any more trouble with Darkie.

* * *

It was soon after this that the Second World War started and we kids were evacuated to Weymouth. Dad went into the Navy and Mum worked as a porteress in Mark Lane underground station (now Tower Hill). I was scared about going to Weymouth because I used to wet the bed every night without fail. As it turned out I needn't have been so worried. The wonderful woman with whom we were billeted had no kids of her own, but she calmly asked us which one of us wet the bed. I was quite embarrassed but in a way relieved that she knew. I owned up at once and gave her my rubber sheet which she put on my bed, making me feel relaxed and comfortable by saying that I was not to worry and that everything would be all right.

I lay in bed praying over and over again, 'Please God don't let me wet the bed.' I stayed awake as long as I could, praying all the time. And I didn't wet the bed that night – or any night ever again. It was wonderful. No kid enjoys it, it's lousy waking up in a wet bed – believe me!

There wasn't much schooling in Weymouth, but there was fun. I got myself a paper round (I've always been able to earn a shilling) and I shared the money with my brothers and friends. Most of it was spent in a shop where they made their own ice-cream. On my paper round I used to get to the newsagents before it opened. When the lady who ran it arrived she had to go to the end of the shop to switch on the lights. That's when I nicked the sweets – which were rationed by then. We could never get enough of them, but our Mum helped us out there. She used to come down once a week and because she worked at the underground station she was on the spot when the man came to refill the chocolate-bar vending machine. Mum emptied her purse – and most of the machine – and brought it all down to us, along with the bundles of fish that the fishmarket porters threw out of the passing trains for her.

We hadn't been at Weymouth long before the Germans started bombing it, so we went back to London in time for the Blitz, spending a lot of our time underground.

Every afternoon Mum took us to the Elephant and Castle tube station so that we could get our beds ready and laid out for the night's bombing. Mum insisted we went right along the line to St John's Wood because the station there was new and much cleaner. Later on we had a Morrison shelter put in the house. We didn't need to wait for the sirens, because our old dog always knew when a raid was coming and ran to the shelter before the sirens sounded.

None of us kids were frightened. It became a way of life, with the extra interest of going through the bomb debris every morning hunting for souvenirs. But Dad said it would have a bad effect on us for life if we stayed in London any longer, so we were evacuated again, this time to Bledlow, a lovely village in Buckinghamshire.

Once again I lost out on my schooling, largely because the local farmers took a liking to me and kept taking me out of school to help them on the land. I was thirteen and a strong boy. One day I took my best girl friend into the little railway halt, knowing there would be nobody around because the only train of the day had come and gone. We started to kiss and cuddle. I was having a wonderful time when all of a sudden I had a crazy feeling which made me hold the girl tight and kiss her in a frenzy. It was out of this world and something special was happening, but I didn't know what. I was wild with excitement and loved the girl more every second. Then my little dick exploded and I felt very empty and sad. 'What the hell has happened?' I thought, 'I must get away from this girl and find out.' I made an excuse about just remembering an errand I hadn't done and ran away from her. Further down the lane, where nobody was about, I put my hand in my pants and it came out sticky. What was it? Wow! I'd come and I was a man. I was so proud and happy that I ran all the way home and up to my room to check that I was right. I shall never forget the pride I felt. I couldn't wait to get back to school and tell my mates.

My other great experience at Bledlow was to meet the great music-hall star Josie Collins who lived there. We had plays and concerts at the school and I could tap dance. So Josie taught me a fabulous song and tap routine for the song 'Johnnie Pedlar' (remember that one?). It went down a treat. I also sang and ballroom danced to the 'Girl in the Alice Blue Gown'. My dancing partner was named Irene Gittings, and I loved her too. I used to be dressed as a sea captain and sang while Irene danced and then we would both dance together. We were really quite professional.

Val Parnell and his wife and Bebe Daniels and Ben Lyon also lived in the village and were marvellous to us kids. We used to think that Val was a cowboy because he was so big, and that Helen his wife was a Red Indian because she was so small and dark and had a big plait down her back. I used to go and help them in their garden and they even named a chicken after me. When Dad came home on leave, looking smashing in his uniform, I took him down to meet them. They got him well merry and ended up having to take us all home by car.

Years later we had a great reunion when I was playing at the London Palladium. I was in Harry Secombe's dressing room one night when Val Parnell came in. Harry asked him to guess where he and I had met before. Parnell named all the world's most famous playgrounds, and then Harry explained who I was and where we had met and Val went nearly mad he was so pleased. 'Hang on there Joe, don't move, I'm getting Mrs Parnell.' And in came Helen Parnell and we did the whole routine all over again. 'Where do we know Joe from?' This time it was Helen who named all those places I hadn't even been to yet, but she couldn't guess. When at last we told her she cried with delight, she was so happy to see me again. We relived those days when I had been a kid with them, pinching apples, making butter and of course playing in those school shows. She was really thrilled and so was I.

When Liberace came backstage one night with Mrs Parnell, everyone crowded round to see him. Helen stopped and told him who I was. We shook hands and he said how pleased he was to meet me. We had a chat and on leaving I said 'Goodnight, Mrs Parnell.'

She stopped me. 'What did you call me?' she said.

Blushing, I answered 'Auntie.'

'That's better,' said Helen. What a lovely lady!

3

A Bob Or Two

I started work on the day I was fourteen. Dad took me to Taylor and Frances, a printing firm in Red Lion Court, Fleet Street, and told me to look the boss straight in the eye and squeeze his hand really hard. I did and I got the job – at 17s. 6d. a week. As we were leaving Dad started laughing. He ruffled my hair and said, 'I'm proud of you son – I thought your eyes were going to pop out of your head.' It was a great moment in my life.

I worked in a cellar lit by naked bulbs and stinking of ink and paper. My first job was to learn to lay the paper on markers so exactly that the machine would print perfectly. I practised with stacks of waste paper for a fortnight before I was allowed to go near a machine that was actually printing something. Each sheet of paper had to be one hundred per cent accurately laid – the tiniest fraction of error would ruin the printing – and you only had a limited time to lay the sheets while the machine was running. It made your fingers ultra-sensitive – probably the start of my success at foreplay!

I was also the errand boy, going out for teas and snuff for the compositors. I was supposed to get twelve teas, but before I went to the café I put three cups on one side. Then I would bring back nine cups and pour a little from each into the three I'd set aside. Of course I'd been given the money for twelve cups. I did the same with the snuff, buying one less than they said but filling the empty box with a little from each of the others. It's surprising how much you can make in a week doing that!

In the tea break I read *No Orchids for Miss Blandish*. I loved it. I played with myself every day at 3.30 pm, book in one hand, cock in the other.

Dad was then on the night shift at the *News of the World*, so we used to meet sometimes as he came to work and I went home. I made my pals at work come out and meet my Dad, telling them that he was like a film star. I was so proud of him with his lovely wavy hair; he was beautiful.

When I started work Dad took me to Alice's, a little café in Fleet Street. He introduced me to the big fat Italian lady who ran it and told her to make sure I had my dinner every day. She looked after me like a son and piled my plate so high I don't know how I ate it all. But I've always had a good appetite – for food and life.

At sixteen I joined the printer's union NATSOPA, the National Society of Operative Printers and

Assistants. That was a great day in our family. Dad and a couple of his mates took me to the Union headquarters and waited for me, Dad saying as always: 'Look them straight in the eyes, boy.' I came out with my union card and we went to the pub used by the Fleet Street NATSOPAs, where they toasted me and I felt really proud. Now I was a man in every sense. With a union card in my pocket.

I moved from Red Lion Court to a nice little firm where they printed margarine wrappers. I liked it there: the machine room was on the ground floor with big windows letting in the daylight, a welcome contrast to the dark cellar I'd left behind me.

I used to take the greaseproof paper home for Mum but brother Peter was always pinching it to sell down East Lane market. He was the greatest for that game, always looking for something to sell – but he was a smashing brother.

My next move was to a real class shop, the Baynard Press in Brixton. Now I was really learning the trade, printing books and using five colours, putting my sensitive fingers to good use laying the paper onto the machine marks. It was a great life, even keeping Freddie Schofield, one of the older boys, company on his duty night fire watching (watching out for incendiary bombs). All the other men's wives used to send a little parcel of food for me then, and it was like going to a party. I loved it.

About this time I became interested in weight lifting. So I went to a foundry and melted down a load of lead and made my first weights. But being a silly young sod I tried to take them home all at once.

From Brixton to Walworth, where we lived then, is a fair old trip on foot especially if you are carrying about a hundredweight. It was ridiculous, but I was determined to get that load home. I had to stop at every window-sill for a rest and when I finally got there I was cattled! But I'd done it. The next day I was lifting those weights, and very proud of myself I was too.

By this time I was into wrestling and boxing. I had my first wrestling lesson when I was fourteen. Dad had a friend called Mike Howly, a lightweight Irish pro wrestler and very tough. Mike took me to the Walworth Men's Institute in Ruskin Street, where I told them I was sixteen. The pros and amateurs could train together at the Institute and Mike took me on the mat and gave me my first lesson.

He was like a limpet. No matter what you did, or how you turned, he was on top. It was then that I learnt that the art of wrestling is to keep relaxed. You only put your strength into any hold or throw when you are actually doing the thing. And then when it's 'on' or 'done', you relax. That's why wrestlers can wrestle for hours.

I met Mike years later when I was on top of the pro game. It was in Leeds, a Relwiskow show. He was in the dressing room talking to the boys when I heard his name. I can't tell you how thrilled I was to meet this man again. I introduced myself, gave him my family's regards and thanked him sincerely for helping me when I was a kid. He was quite surprised to know that I'd carried on, and more than pleased to learn that I was now topping the bill.

I was boxing for the Lynn Boxing Club in South

London and Matt Wells, that great champion from way back, used to train us. He was always cutting our hair so that it didn't go in our eyes and fussing us kids like a mother hen. The day before I was due to fight at Manor Place, Matt said: 'Now don't forget – no liquid, just rinse your mouth out and come to Guy's Hospital (that's where he worked looking after the doctors in the gym) and I'll weigh you in the morning and see what we'll do.' Down to Guy's I went. Matt weighed me and I was within the weight, so he took me to the café and bought me a big steak. 'Now don't forget, no liquid until you're weighed in, that way it cheats the scales a few pounds.'

On the night of the fight I was eleven stone three pounds on the scales: just right. Matt bought me a nice cup of tea. 'Now just relax,' he said. He was smashing. When he was in my corner he told me, 'As soon as you get in the middle, aim a right hand right on his chops, it might work.' It didn't. Back in my corner after the first round Matt started telling me what to do next.

'How about my water?' I said.

'You haven't done anything yet,' said Matt, 'go out there and do some work and when you come back I'll give you some water.'

I did, and I won the bout. The corner man can help you win fights and Matt Wells was the greatest. I'll never forget him.

The Lynn Club put me in for my novice competition, which means you have about three fights in one night and if you win them all you pass on to fight a better class of boy. Some boys don't worry about the novice contest and sometimes fight for years before they go in for one. But most clubs, when they run their own show, put on a novice competition if they think their boy can win. That way they give their own show a boost, plus the local boy wins again. I went in for three, silly bastard that I was – I wasn't good enough. In my first I got through to the final. The second was a police competition (D Division). Their boy was Constable Smith and they put it on just for him to win. I know that, because when I got to the show I went up to look at the cups and medals and there was this huge cup inscribed for 'Constable Smith – best performer of the year'. I thought, 'Blimey, I've got one here.'

I won the first and second bouts and there in the final was dear Constable Smith waiting for me. But I'd watched him and thought I could beat him. He'd got a good left hand and I loved anyone who used to keep sticking out their left. I seemed to be able to get under it and belt them in the belly. After the first round I was thinking this competition was mine. He kept poking out his left and I kept whacking them up in his belly. Come the third round and my Dad had gone to get tea and biscuits when he heard the crowd go mad. My boy's won, he thought. Not on your life, his boy had lost. Nobody had told me that Smithy also had a right hand. It knocked me spark out – one minute I was there, winning, the next I'd lost. I don't remember anything until they got me back to my corner. It turned out this boy had hit me in the temple and after that I didn't feel a thing.

That was on a Thursday night. On the Saturday I was fighting an Eaton Manor boy. Now in those days if you fought a boy from that club you were in for a right fight, they were so fit. I was worried sick: suppose I got knocked out again? We came out of our corners and he hit me on the chin, my special gum shield flew out of my mouth, my head spun round, but I was OK. 'Right, you bastard, you can't knock me out,' I thought. Did we have a fight? It was a smasher and I lost.

Then came my third novice competition at the de Havilland aircraft factory. Once again it was set up for a boy belonging to the factory. Very tall he was, with a good left hand. We both reached the final. When I came back to my corner after the first round Frank Duffy, my second, said, 'What are you doing, Joe? Letting him win? You're not doing anything. Go out there and beat him.' Frank won that competition for me – out I went and beat the fellow.

So at last I was an intermediate boxer, and the Club Secretary Mr Tucker, who was there to see me fight, congratulated me by hitting me on the chin with such enthusiasm that he nearly knocked me out! I was so happy – even though I couldn't eat for a couple of days.

When I wasn't at the print or boxing I was having fun – and on the lookout for an extra bob or two. One day George, a pal of mine, asked me if I'd like to earn a few quid with him.

'Sure I would.'

'You know I work in the tarpaulin yard, well, there's some really big ones there and I know someone who will buy them.'

'What do you want me to do?' I asked.

'Well, there's a horse and cart there. You drive it and we'll split the profit,' he said.

'Lovely,' was my response.

We went on a Sunday morning, the day the yard was shut. My pal got in and opened the gates, I got the horse and cart (it was more like a covered wagon) and drove in and he closed the doors behind me. The horse shit in the yard and, God knows why, I cleaned it up and put the mess in the wagon. It just shows you what amateur thieves we were, cleaning up the horse-shit so that nobody'd know we'd been there. Yet in no time those eighty-foot tarpaulin sheets that had been hanging there were gone. Crazy! We got the sheets down and folded them up but they were so big we could only get two in the wagon. We closed the yard up and went on our way. There was a hump-backed bridge off Albany Road, called Addington Bridge. Nobody told me that when you go over a hump-backed bridge with a horse and cart you're supposed to put your foot on the brake to stop the cart running back. I didn't, and the shafts shot up in the air nearly taking the horse with them. I went over backwards, frightened to death, but I had the sense to grab the brake that held up the cart, allowing the horse to pull us over the bridge. If anyone did see us, they must have thought it was cowboys and Indians – me the cowboy driving hell for leather down the road with the Indians after me. The adrenalin was running high when I swung the horse and cart into the yard where we were to unload, nearly knocking half the house down doing it; and after all that I think the man gave us all of a tenner for the two tarpaulins. We must have been mad; but the excitement was wonderful.

* * *

Nowadays I'm so glad that I loved and respected my Mum and Dad like I did. I stopped doing these rackets in case I got caught and brought disgrace upon them. Loving them saved me from a life of crime, which was what a lot of my school friends went into. They're richer than me now, but what the hell!

4

In And Out Of The Army

Home life was great but I wanted to get out into the world, so I was eager to do my National Service. Dad was still in the Navy and that's where I really wanted to be. But it was easier at the time to get into the Army so that's where I went. I passed my medical A1 and really looked forward to going in. Mum cried but Dad, strong as ever, just said: 'Do your best, boy, and make us proud of you.' I've always tried to do that, Dad.

I went to Brentwood for my six weeks primary training, and I loved every minute of it. It was hard and physical – marching, assault courses, forced marches, exercise with rifles – right up my street. It was like being in the gymnasium every day, all day. During our training we had to do a monkey run, which is running along on your hands and knees –

battle training, they call it. Our instructor made a race of it. I had to go over a load of pebblestones and I knew I just had to get there first. And I did. But my knees were skinless and pouring with blood and I wound up in hospital for two weeks. I didn't care. When I came out they told me I had to be relegated because I had lost two of the six weeks training. Was I choked? I liked the crowd of fellows I was with and didn't want to leave them. I persuaded my sergeant to agree that if I learnt about the weapons, machine-guns and the rest in double quick time I could stay with the crowd. When the others were off duty I kept going and practised for hours with the guns and the armoury. Blindfolded, I'd take them apart and put them together again until I mastered the lot. All the physical tests were easy for me, so I was able to stay on the course and pass it and was posted to the artillery.

So off to Dover Castle I went to learn about 6-inch and 15-inch coastal guns. Dummy loading 6-inch shells all day was great. The shells weighed 50 to 60 lbs and we had to practise loading false guns, by hand of course. What a sweat and how I loved it. I enjoyed Dover, too. The gymnasium was outside the castle on the edge of the cliffs. When our squad had just started exercising in the gym, Lance Bombardier Stan Ramsell passed by me. I was jumping up and down. 'Don't I know you?' he asked. I stopped jumping up and down. 'Keep going,' he said. Stan was a keen PT instructor. So up and down I went as I was speaking to him. It turned out we did know each other from mutual friends and boxing. Stan was a great international boxer from the Keys Boxing

Club. I was just a beginner, having a fight now and then.

'Come down to the gym tonight,' he said, 'we're going to have some sparring.'

'Sure, but I'm on kitchen fatigues first.'

'That's okay, come after you have finished your duties.'

After fatigues I went to the gymnasium and to my surprise there were one or two top brass there. But before I could retreat Stan saw me.

'Hello,' he said, 'get the gloves on.'

I didn't know how to get out of there fast enough. Stan must have thought I was yellow. But when I explained to him later that I had pinched tins of peaches and other goods from the kitchen and they were all stuck in my trousers and loose denims, we had a good laugh about it. I could just imagine being ordered: 'Gunner Cornelius, strip for boxing,' and tins of fruit falling all over the ring. I'd have got at least a month in the glasshouse.

Training finished, Stan recommended me to go into the gym as an Acc 1 – Assistant Instructor. I had to go to Shoreham for my PT course and if I passed it I'd be Lance Bombardier. My instructor on this course was Staff Sergeant Webb of the Army Physical Training Corps. He was a bastard to us. It was the toughest course I had ever been on. It was death drop, death walk, death slide, death this and death that and, believe me, it frightened the bloody life out of me. At one time I told Mum and Dad I thought I would desert. Most of these death things were to do with heights and I cannot stand heights, even though

I started climbing everything in sight when I was three. I'll never forget the death drop. You had a toggle around your waist, with a steel ring. Through the ring you had two ceiling ropes. You climbed a rope ladder and when you reached the roof you hit it to let Webby know that you were really at the top. Then you held the ropes while they took the ladder away. After that the boys on the floor, three on each rope, would walk away leaving you up in the air just resting with the steel ring on the V of the two ropes. And you had to be in the right position, which meant to attention, toes pointed, hands clasped behind your back – forty feet up in the air and just the V of the two ropes holding you. When Webby was satisfied you were all correct, he gave a sign and the boys on the ropes ran together and you dropped. When Webby gave a shout again, the boys stood and pulled and you stopped. When it happened to me they all laughed. My feet actually touched the floor. 'I think you've gone grey, Cornelius,' said Webby.

'I think I've shit myself,' I replied. I don't know if that performance helped me pass, but I was one of the five out of fifteen who became Acc 1's.

The night before the results the boys were in a right state. Webby was such a bastard none of us thought we had passed. Usually you bought the instructor a present on the last night, and none of us was sure whether we wanted to or not. It was decided that I would break into the office by a window in the gymnasium and see if I could find the results. I did get in and I found them. Needless to say Webby didn't get any present. But I think he was so tough because he knew that only those who had the guts to go through it all would pass. I met him later at the Army Physical Training Corps at Aldershot. He suddenly seemed quite a nice fellow. I suppose it was because we were by then on equal footing, for now I was a sergeant in the Army Physical Training Corps.

Back to Dover I went as an Acc 1 with a red-and-black striped jersey. I moved into where Stan Ramsell stayed in the barracks on the second floor, with windows overlooking the sea. There was a long dormitory with about twenty beds, all shared by NCOs. The lavatories were on the floor below and one night when I wanted a wee, but didn't want to go downstairs (it must have been about two o'clock in the morning) I got up in the window, opened it and started to let go. Poor Stan woke up and screamed, thinking I was a vampire or a ghost, while the wind was blowing the piss all over him. I did laugh about it – afterwards! We were great pals, Stan and I. He was so serious, but liked to needle me at times. Then, when I got rattled, he'd say: 'Lost your temper, haven't you?' And that would make me worse.

One night in the NAAFI, the piano was playing and I was singing and getting quite excited, banging the table when, without thinking, I threw my tea all over Stan. His face went white. 'You're losing your temper, aren't you?' I said. I was as near to a fight with Stan as I'd ever been. But I think he knew that if he whacked me I wouldn't let the NAAFI girls have my body so that he could get his extra fag ration.

I used to take the NAAFI girls down to our gym. The boys on guard duty would leave and we would make love on the mats. Next day the boys would get extra fags and I would get chocolate. I often told Stan he started his business up on the money he saved (which was fourteen shillings a week) while I spent all my money and sold my body for his fags.

The recruits used to like my PT classes because we were always larking about and when we went on runs outside the castle I would let them lie down in the sun while Stan made his boys keep going. Then when it was time to run in my boys were always in straight lines and looking great. It paid off for me.

One day the colonel was standing on the outside of the gymnasium as we ran in. I spotted him and said to the lads: 'Come on fellas, we're being watched, play the game.' And we came in like the best trained soldiers you have ever seen.

Soon after that I was recommended to the Army Physical Training Corps at Aldershot, where I did six months murderous physical training which I loved. I learnt so much and was so proud to belong to the corps. I had a great instructor. I think that without him I would never have passed the exam.

It was short hair at that school and of course I had the longest hair you have ever seen. After our first afternoon the instructor spoke to me, 'Son, if you want to get through this course, I'd get that hair cut because if you don't everyone will be picking on you.' I thought about how nicely he had put it to me, made a decision and went straight round to the camp barber. 'Take the fucking lot off,' I said. When I got back to the barracks no one recognised me, I looked a proper skinhead.

When we went to the company swimming pool, we had to change up on the balcony floor and jump over the balcony into the pool. Now I wasn't a bad swimmer, but there was no way I could do that, being scared of heights. The instructor came up to me while I had one leg over the rail, feeling a right pratt, and said: 'What's the matter Cornelius?'

'Sorry Staff, I can't stand heights.'

He didn't push me or relegate me. He took me to the diving board which was that much lower. I tried, I ran along the board – and stopped. I turned sideways, stood on the edge and shut my eyes. No good, I just couldn't go. I was sick of myself. Here I was training to be an Army Physical Training Corps Instructor, and making a right muck-up. But the instructor knew his job. He took me to the side of the bath and said jump. I felt a right nana but I jumped, and it wasn't so bad. In about two weeks I was as near to the roof as I could be, jumping in and loving every minute of it. So much so that I volunteered for the paratroopers when the course was over.

About one hundred men started the course and about forty finished. Now I was a sergeant and my first post was at the Guards depot at Colchester. I went with Georgie Williams, another good amateur boxer. We duly arrived with our new white stripes, new flashes, and new crossed swords. We were going to show them how physical training should be done. Through the gates, a big guardsman slammed to attention and directed us to the guard house, even though we asked for the gymnasium. And then the biggest RSM you ever saw told us in no uncertain terms that we would not interfere with the way the Acc 1's ran the classes. We would only make sure that the exercises were correct. What we saw was an eye-opener. For six months we had been taught: do not boss, do not order, coax the men to do exercises – and here were Acc 1's hitting the men, kicking them up the arse and all sorts. The Guards' training was really strict and tough. They weren't allowed outside the barracks for the first three months. By the end of that time they were one hundred per cent guardsmen.

From Colchester I was sent to Saighton Camp, Chester. There were about ninety APTC instructors there, all fit and strong and game for anything. Every Friday night there was a dance for the NCOs and all the local girls, who liked nice fit fellows, used to come to the dance hoping to be obliged. They were, in no uncertain terms! We all lived in 'spiders' – long dormitories partitioned off into small rooms.

So Friday night it was curtains drawn, big fire up the chimney, making the room like a sauna, French letters under the pillow and when the girls arrived they didn't stand a chance. Some mornings the boys on guard duty would knock on my window and say, 'It's okay, Sarge, we've let the girls out' and I'd let them off PT that day. It was a good life.

It was about this time that I fell in love – as I often did. When I went home on leave this girl friend, Paula, took me to her Auntie's place for dinner. And there was this large room with a lovely blazing fire and a very large bed. While we were eating my eyes kept straying to the bed in the corner. So I asked Paula to marry me. Things were so different in those days!

Because I was only nineteen, I had to ask my parents' permission. Dad immediately said no. Good old Dad. And I wish my lovely Mum had listened to him. But she convinced Dad to let me go ahead, and I didn't help matters by saying that if I didn't get their agreement I would go to my commanding officer and get his permission, which would be enough as I was a sergeant. (Bloody fool I was.)

I remember the wedding day, looking beautiful in my Army dress suit, with crossed swords and stripes freshly whitened. We got married in Walworth Town Hall. After the ceremony we had to run for the bus, covered in confetti, because I had no money. We went home to Mum's food and then back to Auntie's big bed for the initiation. It was lovely. But I won't say any more about Paula because, as you can see, she had nothing to do with my Army life.

The boys in the camp, for some soppy reason, had to wear army boots when they went out of the camp. It didn't matter whether they had bad feet or not, boots were the order even if they were going out in civvies or to a dance. So the boys took their shoes out in a small pack and changed away from the camp. I was in the mess one night when I got a message. A couple of recruits wanted to see me. Out I went and found that the sergeant in charge of the guard that night had given orders that all small packs were to be searched and if shoes were found the men were to be put on a charge. So the poor sods were all hanging around a coffee stall outside the camp, afraid to come in. I took all the small packs I could carry and brought them inside. The sergeant in charge heard what I was doing and came to see me. He was a snidey little sod.

'Cornelius, what are you doing?'

'What does it look like, you stupid bastard?'

He didn't know what to say and lamely replied, 'Put your hat on straight – you idiot.'

I put my hat on straight and told him I'd see him in the wash-room in the morning, which I did. I held him up against the toilets and threatened to punch his soppy head in if he ever had a go at me again, and I told him to leave the boys alone. It all passed over, he was an idiot anyway.

When all the sergeants from the camp went into Chester, the locals must have thought we were mad. All these young sods back-flipping, hand-springing and hand-balancing, down the main road. But we were just young and fit. The locals were not afraid to walk down the High Street; they knew we wouldn't dream of being disrespectful to them.

But the fun was soon to go out of my life. Because I'd done so well in anatomy and physiology, they sent me to convalescent and development centres and I began to lose my love of the Army. It was so dull for me to be more of a clerk than a PT instructor. I just had to watch young men doing exercises that would straighten their bodies and make them fit again. I know now what a great job it was, but at the time I was fit, young and impatient and it was all too slow. I used to get the best results in class by asking the boys 'Who has made love to a girl?'

A few would hold their hands up giggling and I would say 'Right, everybody grab an arse.'

Then I'd say 'Right, let's go through the motions – as if we are fucking.'

It was the best abdominal and spinal exercise you have ever seen: backs quickly became straight as a die.

So much so that one poor sod I'd taken to the doctor must have been doing extra, because his back was going the other way. So we let him go on normal duties and he left the centre A1.

Most of the boys had hollow backs, flat feet, humpty backs or curvature of the spine. They were taken into the army in a low grade and then sent to us to cure their deformities and make them A1 in eight weeks if possible. And invariably we did.

About this time one of the old soldiers was caught messing around with a young recruit. This kid wet the bed and the old soldier had kidded the boy that he had a remedy to stop him doing it. He was a tough old sod and a dirty bastard. I had to stay in his room with him to guard him, as it were, until morning when he would be court-martialled.

I was very young myself in those days, nineteen in fact, and I was a little bit worried about going to sleep. I warned him, if he so much as came anywhere near me, I'd knock his bloody head off! He just went to sleep, of course, but I was very pleased when morning came and the Military Police took him away. You never know, he could have raped me! And that's a laugh!

The discipline suddenly became too much for me and I became a rebel. I really gave the squaddies an easy time. One week I was on gymnasium duty, which meant a fatigue team would come each night to polish the place from top to bottom. Some gyms used to paint the knobs on their medicine balls red and the game lines white because the smartest gymnasium received a plaque each week. What a lot of cobblers! On the last night before the inspection you had a whole platoon to really give it that final go. By the time the boys had finished giving me their excuses – meeting birds and the like – I wound up with about five instead of twenty men to do the gym from top to bottom. I had a brainwave. We got the hose and flooded the gym, up the walls, over the windows, everywhere. I sent one of the boys off to the dining room to get some food and he brought back the biggest lump of bread and cheese you ever saw. Christ, it looked so awful I just put it in the cupboard. Everything was finished in record time and we were all very pleased with ourselves. It was dark now, all shining and lovely, so off to the mess I went very happy.

But in the cold light of day the gymnasium looked bloody awful, streak lines of dirt where the water had been swept away, the windows all lines – blimey was I in trouble. The Major in charge of the whole camp came around with his entourage and when he saw the place he went spare. The first place he looked was in the cupboard and there was my lump of bread and cheese looking at him. Was he mad. The Sergeant Major asked the Major if he could speak to me in private. The Major agreed but by this time I had had enough of all the bullshit and before the Sergeant Major could tick me off I called him a cunt, said he couldn't run a gym, couldn't run people, he could go fuck himself and the Army as well. So of course I got court-martialled.

But it wasn't so bad. I think the Major used to like me because the club I boxed for in Chester, which was run by Gunner Moore, the old knuckle fighter, sent him a letter asking if I could box at the Liverpool

Stadium. The Major, not knowing about my boxing, was quite surprised and called me in to ask about it and to see if I would box for the Army. After the court martial he took me to one side and said, 'Cornelius, you and the Sergeant Major are like dogs. Sometimes two dogs can meet and just sniff each other's arses, but another two dogs will meet and start a fight – just like you and the Sergeant Major. So – I will move you to another Company.'

'Thank you, Sir,' I said. In the meantime, I went back to Company D and found that the Sergeant Major wanted to talk to me.

'I don't want to talk to you,' I said, but he persuaded me to go back to his office and talk it over.

'Look,' he said, 'let's not be silly, let's try and get along.' He suggested that he get me an eighty-four hour leave and asked if I would use part of it to visit his wife in London. I was only too happy to have leave and quite happy to look in on his wife for him. We ended up good pals and I went to the Major and said that I had learnt my lesson, that I was getting on with the Sergeant Major quite well and that I wanted to stay in D company. He agreed and from then on life was pretty good.

At the camp there was also another Sergeant Major who was a great ballroom dancer. Every Thursday night I would go down to the gym and take lessons. I loved it and really got into it. I learnt easily. The Sergeant Major's wife would take me round and then I'd dance the woman's part and by then I'd have it. It was smashing, especially as all the ATS girls wanted to partner a good dancer.

I'd always jived and jitterbugged before and when I was out of the Army, up to the Lyceum I went and forgot all about ballroom dancing and went back to jiving. It's a pity really because I'd got quite good at it; but all my pals in Civvy Street weren't into that square stuff. Shame!

From Saighton Camp I went to Richmond Park and that was a lovely post. I had my own room and went home every night. It was a convalescent depot right in the middle of the park, and once again slow but good work. If only I could have liked it and had the sense to make the most of it – and if only I had that chance all over again.

While I was in Richmond Park I used to catch the 7.30 am workman's train up to work and the 4.30 pm train back. On the night of the weekly dance, I was, as far as my wife was concerned, on duty. And was I having a ball? All those unfit, unwell chaps and me, a raring to go PTI.

But I wasn't there long before I got my demob. First I went on a demob course. What a bloody young fool I was. I went on a six-week printer's course that didn't teach me a thing, just because it was around the corner from my one-room flat and I could be at home nights.

I could have taken a six-month physiotherapist's course and qualified, then my low education grades would not have stopped me from getting into the one field I should now so dearly love to work in. But when you're young, you just don't think, do you?

5

A Love Lesson

Back in Civvy Street, I lived with Paula in my Uncle George and Aunt Vi's house, two up, two down, off the Old Kent Road. They were great to live with. Although they didn't have much they certainly made the most of what they did have and they were always laughing and joking. It was also back to the print. I became a jobber in Fleet Street, which meant I had no regular work but, with the other youngsters, used to sign on all the papers on the Street hoping that one of them would give me a day or night's work. Still, even when we weren't working we were enjoying ourselves.

We used to hang around the Press café and the Blackfriars milk bar – the black and white one that was on the corner of Blackfriars Street and Fleet Street. We called it Poverty Corner because so often we didn't even have the price of a cup of tea. But soon we sorted out the girls who worked there and kidded many a free cup of tea or coffee out of them. I fancied one of the girls at the milk bar. She was more mature than the others and surprised me one day by inviting me round to her flat. Around I went, telling my wife I was looking for work. Up till then I'd just been chatting up this girl who was called Alice. I hadn't even kissed her. But when I knocked on her door she pulled me in and stuck her tongue so far down my throat I was quite taken aback. She was so sure of herself and she didn't waste any time. We got together and started kissing and cuddling, and when I broke away she said, 'I know what you want!' and led me to the bedroom like a lamb to the slaughter. I started fucking and as I began to get really excited she quietened me down, saying, 'Shush, steady, slowly baby. That's right, take your time, here – let me kiss you,' and down she went.

I thought I knew all about making love but it turned out I knew nothing. She was short, big-breasted and had a beautiful arse. We played and made love all night and she would never let me come until she was ready to finish. It was a wonderful lesson. Thanks, Alice, you taught me so well that you've made a lot of other girls happy.

Years later I met Alice again one lunchtime in a pub. I took her home and started making love, but she broke away and fetched her camera. When she'd made my cock stand really well she took a picture of it. She always did surprise me – I've often wondered if she kept a collection of photographs of all the cocks that had fucked her – but she was really nice.

* * *

Soon after that first night I spent with Alice, the milk bar decided to put in a new manageress. I suppose it was because we jobbers were drinking away all the profits. The newcomer was small, dark, wore glasses and she was tough. She wouldn't let us chat up the girls or even hang around the place. The free teas and coffees dried up. We had almost decided to pack in the place when my pal, Terry, a good-looking boy, decided to try making a fuss of her. It worked. She fell overboard for him and we all jumped on the bandwagon and played up to her. The free teas and coffees started coming across again.

Those were the days when it was easy to get hold of duty-free watches and sell them on at quite a profit. The trouble was that after a while so many people had bought them that the bottom fell out of the market. One day when I was stuck with a watch, I went into the milk bar and asked the manageress if she'd like to buy it. 'I haven't got time now,' she said, 'but if you bring it round to my flat about eight o'clock, I'll buy it.'

So round I went – and she opened the door in her nightdress!

'You're early,' she said. 'I told you nine o'clock, but it doesn't matter. Come on in, I was just having a wash.'

I thought to myself, 'Hello, why am I going into the bedroom?'

The fire was blazing and she was sitting on the edge of the bed washing her little legs. Naturally the housecoat was to one side and she was showing quite a lot, and of course I got very fruity. It wasn't long before we were in bed together and by the time I left she had bought the watch. After that, whenever I was stuck with a watch I used to go round to see her. I never did find out what she did with all those watches, but she certainly did buy a few, bless her.

I used to sell quite a lot of things in the print in those days, swag mostly. I never knew what I was going to buy when I went every day to the Houndsditch warehouse or the wholesale shops in Petticoat Lane. But I finished up by having about five fellows working for me at each paper. They used to come to my flat where I had one room filled up with goodies and they took them sale or return. If they sold them they paid me, if not they brought them back. I had a good thing going then and I should have finished up a very rich man. But I never did, of course. All my wives and divorces took my money. At this time I was going around with a great pal called Sid Charlesworth, one of a well-loved market family and a fantastic boxer. Sid had a good line in carrier bags. I used to help him make them – by handing him the studs! Sid had a stall in East Lane, where he sold all kinds of bags. Today he has a beautiful shop in the Lane selling skin bags and marble tables and lamps.

Some weeks I took a stall myself and sold my swag. Once, on a Sunday, I had a load of plastic trumpets and I could really knock out a tune on them. I was blowing away and it seemed that everybody in the market was listening, when I suddenly realised it was 11 o'clock on Remembrance Day. I felt terrible. But I sold all my trumpets!

East Lane was a fantastic, energetic hub of activity. The stalls had been passed down from generation to

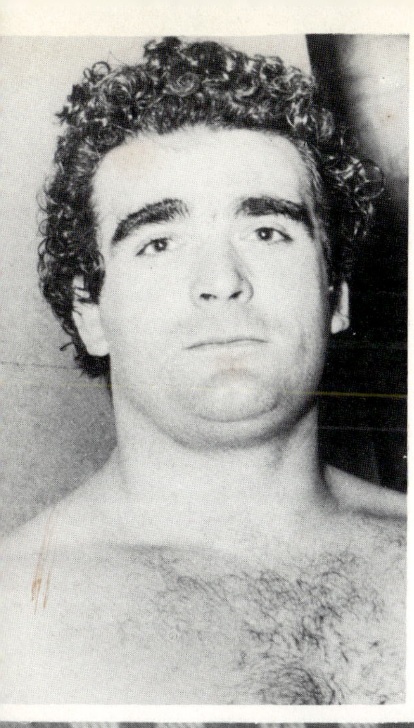

Joe Cornelius, the new Southern area heavyweight champion.

Early boxing days – at Manor Place Baths, Walworth.
(H. W. Neale)

'My gov'nor' – Tony Mancelli, the man who made me. *(S. N. Wilson)*

Right Lou Marco, the greate ref of them all. *(S. N. Wilson*

Cor Argentino giving the fan hard time in Antwerp. *(Eigen Foto)*

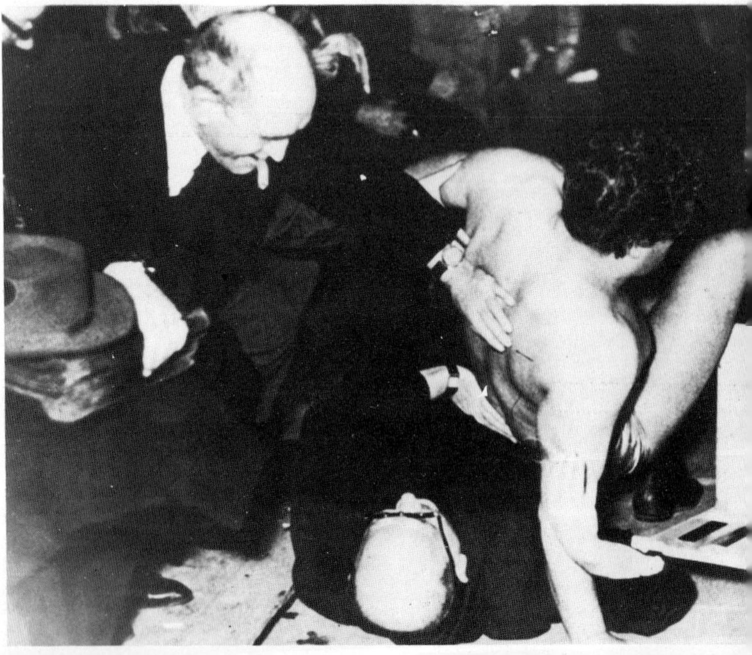

I jump the ring to challenge Bert Assiratti. *('Ace' News Photo Feature Agency)*

Assiratti the greatest gets a taste of my drop-kick – the beginning of the end for me . . .

. . . The end in sight.

The fight with Robert Duranton that put my knee out – and began my stage career! *(Poster, Ghent Coliseum)*

As hard as they come – Beryl Reid tests her muscle-man.

Posing with the Palladium dancing girls.

generation and all the stallholders knew each other. The long, narrow road with stalls on each side was packed with people, shoulder to shoulder. Thousands thronged the market every weekend, greeting each other round the jellied eel stall or the sarsaparilla stand. You could buy anything down there, and I mean anything. Quite a lot of commodities seem to fall off the back of lorries and find their way down to the Lane. The pubs were always full and the pianos were always playing like mad. It seemed that everybody in South London was there. You could hear people calling to each other, laughing and joking – everyone knew everyone. The three pubs overflowed with folk and there was always somebody to get on the mike and sing. The Mason's Arms was always my favourite, where all the families got together while mum put the dinner on and nipped out to join them once it was safe in the oven. East Lane was special: a lovely warm, exciting place as I hope it will remain for many years to come.

It was my Uncle George who persuaded me to start boxing again. I was twenty-one and I'd been absent from the amateur ring for a long time.

I went to the Fitzroy Boxing Club and asked them to fix me up with a fight. They did – against a lad from the great boxing family of Bebington. I thought they were taking liberties with me, putting me on with such an experienced fighter when I'd only just come back into the ring. So I told all my friends that I would go down in the third round.

Came the night of the fight and we both started quietly in the first round, taking it easy as we sized each other up. But in the second, Bebington caught me off balance and knocked me down. I thought, 'Now I'm down, I might as well stay down. I was going to anyway in the third, why not now?' So down I stayed. It was the longest time I'd ever lain on a floor. I thought they'd never come and get me. They were waiting for me to get up, I suppose.

I got my fruit bowl as a consolation prize, but my pals made me suffer, especially Stan Ramsell, my boxing mate. 'You must be mad,' he said. 'You were doing so well up to that soppy fall.' I was disgusted with myself. God knows what made me do it or why I was so stupid.

I was so mad at myself that I went to the club and told them to set me up a fight every week and I'd knock them all out. And I meant it. I'd shown myself up and disgraced the family name which means everything to me. I'd now got the killer instinct – which you need when you box. I was going to go in and fight my heart out.

The club got the message and fixed me up to fight the following week at Bermondsey Baths. I don't remember the fellow's name now, but I swear I'd have killed him – or died trying. Then fate took a hand in the shape of my Uncle Ben and cousin Phillip. I met them in the family pub, The Station, in John Ruskin Street. Uncle Ben said, 'Let's all have a good drink.'

'No thanks,' I said, 'I'm boxing at Bermondsey soon.'

But my Uncle Ben was a right character and wouldn't take no for an answer. So I said, 'Look, if we're going to have a drink I won't, but if we're going to get pissed I will.'

And we did – pissed as puddings, the three of us. So I never got to Bermondsey. I wonder what would have happened to me if I had carried on boxing? I might have been a champion or a punch-drunk has-been. So many ifs in my life.

6

On My Way

I was still working in the print when a wrestling friend asked, 'Why don't you turn pro?'

'No, I'm not good enough,' I replied flatly.

He explained that he knew Toni Mancelli, a great pro wrestler, and fixed a meeting for us in a pub in the Cut (a famous market street in London) one Sunday lunchtime. When I arrived, a woman at the piano was singing 'How Much is that Doggie in the Window?'. I shall never forget that song because that morning Toni and I sealed a lifetime's friendship. We got as drunk as sacks, sang our hearts out and I got home about 6.30 pm. My dinner was put in front of me and it was black. I started to eat, too drunk to taste anything. My wife allowed me a few mouthfuls and then took the plate away and put me to bed. And that was the beginning of my wonderful friendship with Toni, and a lifetime's work in the wrestling ring.

A week later Toni took me to a gym over Mick Casey's Dance Hall at the Elephant and Castle. Toni and Mick proceeded to knock seven kinds of shit out of me to see if I was good enough for the pro business. In those days I was young and fit and you had to practically tear my head off before I would submit. Believe me, they tried to make me. I nearly got punch drunk in that session alone. Later I learned that he who fights and runs away, lives to fight another day.

After that gruelling session, Toni asked George Williams, a good amateur and pro wrestler, to take me to Toni Mansie's gym at Mount Pleasant. There I met not only Mansie, but that great wrestler Joe D'Orazio. I shall always be grateful for all the help they gave me, including the black eyes and busted nose I collected from them in training. Joe was promoting at the time and had helped a wrestler called Ray Appollon, who couldn't get a fight in this country. Joe fixed him up with a couple of bouts, and then Ray went to Germany. While he was out there Ray sent for Joe who was wanted for a fight. Joe couldn't leave his fish and chip shop, but he sent the promoters pictures of an up-and-coming boy – me!

And that's how the lad who'd never been abroad before found himself in Berlin as a fully-fledged pro wrestler. I went out there with Toni Mansie and the promoters made a big fuss of us. They took us to a hotel and told us the set-up. In Germany at that time all the wrestlers paraded around the ring, were introduced to the crowd and then paired off for that night's fights. This was to be a three-month competition. We would wrestle in the same hall every night until finally everyone was eliminated except the winner. It turned out to be fabulous for me, because what I learnt one night I would try out the night after, which was a great way to learn the business. I had never seen such big men before – giants of all shapes. I looked like a baby against them, weighing only about thirteen stone. But I always led the march of the gladiators around the ring and I got a great reception. When your name was called out, you would step forward and the audience would acclaim you and, to my astonishment, give you presents! A wrestler was a god in those days. I used to get a lot of champagne, so I put all the corks on a string and wound them around the corner post. I'm not silly!

When I entered the ring for my first match I was given a rousing reception, but I was scared out of my life. I'd never had a pro fight before, and these giants were veterans with busted eyes, broken noses and cauliflower ears. The promoter and the wrestlers thought I was a fully-fledged professional, and because I was such a good-looking fellow the boys decided they were going to make all kinds of mincemeat out of me. I thought 'Here we go!'

The bell sounded and a giant lumbered out to me and threw me off the ropes but, to his surprise, I somersaulted, landed on my feet, jumped up and drop-kicked him right in the face. The crowd went mad. He got up and Irish-whipped me – taking my arm out straight, spinning under it, whipping the arm round and spinning me over him in a throw. I rolled to my feet, jumped up on his shoulders, legs around his neck tight, threw myself into a somersault, whipping him over my body to the floor. The crowd were standing up, going crazy. He got up, punched me in the balls, kicked me on the floor and was disqualified. He ran out of the ring, mad at me. I was still on the floor holding my balls. They hadn't seen this kind of work before. Up till then it had been all slow Graeco-Roman type of wrestling with plenty of straining. This was new. I even had the boys guessing, and it did the trick. I was a winner with the crowd and, although the other fighters used to give me a good thumping now and again when they could hold me down, I was on my way to the top. My confidence grew and so did my name, although it took me all my time to remember it. For some reason the promoters billed me as William Willard, USA, and after matches, with the public waiting outside for autographs, I was always asking Ray Appollon, 'What's my name?' But it was great – I was the Adonis of Berlin. I used to sing in the clubs. The boys said, 'You have to drag him up and then you have to drag him off!' I always love to sing a song and in Germany, of course, if I didn't know the words, I made them up. Nobody understood me anyway.

While I was there I had an affair with a girl who had come from the Russian sector. She used to make me feel like a million dollars, such a fantastic lover! We'd be at it, I'd put it in and she'd climb up the bed, moaning and groaning. I was a little bit confused though because I couldn't feel the sides of her tunnel. One day I overheard her and her cousin discussing whom she would blame for the baby. I knew it was time to go back to England. I'd only come to Berlin for ten days originally but had stayed a couple of months and gone through three-quarters of my fights, winning them all. The promoters asked me to stay, so I wrote to my wife asking her to come to Berlin. But she, not knowing the great success I'd made, couldn't make it out, and didn't write and didn't come. I thought I had better go and find out what was happening at home. I had a little trouble with the promoters, because they didn't want me to go, but I promised to come straight back. They gave me a contract and I returned home – the big conquering hero.

I decided not to tell my wife and just arrive and surprise her. I got off the bus, walked down Albany Road and whistled up to my back window as I always did. The window went up and my wife was shouting, 'Where have you been, you no-good sod? Don't you come here, I don't want you. Piss off!'

I was shocked! Me! The big wrestler! What a homecoming!

I went round to the front of the building and the window was opened.

'Don't you come up here, piss off, we don't want you.'

I was feeling sick now. I didn't say a word. I ran up the stairs, all eighty-four of them, carrying my cases as well, found the door to the flat was open, but no one was there. I went down the long passage into the lounge and there were my wife and son, George.

'Don't you come in here,' she screamed at me. 'Go wherever you've been, we don't want you.'

I stood there in shock. Then I moved towards her and slapped her face.

'You never answered my letter,' I said, 'I was waiting for you to come out. What do you think I am?'

She fell into my arms. Finally she cooked me a lovely meal and then sat on my lap. Georgie was asleep and some neighbours came in to see me. She told them, 'Go away, he's mine today.' So they left and she took me to bed. What a lovely life!

A few days later I went to Wimbledon Palais to see some of the wrestling boys and was offered a contract to go to India. I was so excited, I rushed straight home. 'I'm going to India,' I announced proudly.

'Oh no you're not! If you go, don't come back, I'll leave if you go.'

So I didn't go. I didn't go back to Germany either – I went back to the print.

I told Toni Mancelli all about my trip and how well I'd done and asked for some fights in England. At that time there weren't many chances for new boys. There wasn't much work about and the very small circle of wrestlers in the heavyweight division wanted to keep out the newcomers. I kept nagging Toni until the day came when I was in his flat and the phone rang. When he put it down he said to me, 'So you want work?'

'Yes, when are you going to get me some?'

'Go home and pack your bag.'

'What?'

'Do you want to work?'

'Yes.'

'OK, you're in Ipswich tonight.'

'Who am I on with?'

'I don't know. Go home and I'll pick you up.'

I ran home and packed all my togs which were cleaned and ironed, just waiting to be used. We got to Ipswich – and I still didn't know who I was with.

It turned out that Al Hayes, who was on with Toni, had broken his leg and I was taking his place. Toni was laughing his head off. 'Now we'll see just how good you are and what you learnt in Germany,' he said. I was determined to show him just how good I was. When the bout started, we were like two flies buzzing around the ring. For heavies, we were moving like lightweights. In the third round, Toni cut my eye so badly that the eyebrow was hanging down and I was looking over the top of it. But Toni didn't ease up. I think he had a two-day growth of beard and he kept rubbing it on my eyebrow to keep the blood flowing – which it did. The ring was red, I was red, Toni was red because I never left him or slowed down, wanting to show him I could take and give it. He beat me on a fall after five ten-minute rounds. It was a great fight, the crowd loved it, Toni was pleased with me and I was truly happy. I'd made it in Berlin and now I knew I'd made it in England, because Toni was the best and I was his protégé. I knew too that he was proud of me and that plenty of work would follow – as it did. The wrestling world is a small world where news travels fast, and our bout was already on the grapevine to the promoters. I had to have ten stitches in my eyebrow and my eye was black; but I was as proud as a peacock, and Toni got a real telling off from his wife Lilli for injuring me!

* * *

Toni proceeded to get me work in Liverpool Stadium, Blackpool Tower and Belle Vue, Manchester: three of the biggest arenas in England and jealously guarded by the top heavyweights as their very own territory. Only the very best got there and now that I was there too, I was a very proud young man.

Toni warned me, 'Joe, sometime, someone will have a right go at you. When that happens, revert to the cobbles and fight, because the game is so small that if you swallow it, they will all go in to smash you up. Don't forget what I've told you. If you think anyone is popping you – kill 'em.'

For my first fight I was in Liverpool and on with Bill McDonald, a great man and a fantastic showman. We were in and out of the ring like yo-yos. We had a smashing fight but when I got back to my hotel I was black and blue. When my blood had cooled down I was really in pain. My head in particular was killing me. I suppose I'd tried too hard in the ring that night. I ran a hot bath and soaked. It was the worst thing I could have done, because it helped bring out the bruises.

I should have left it for a while. I never slept a wink that night. The next day I was in Manchester, at Belle Vue. Mancelli was on the same bill. When he met me at the station he said, 'What the hell is wrong with you? You look awful.'

So I told him how I'd been in with Bill McDonald and how I'd been in and out of the ring and how I'd hurt myself a few times on the ring apron. Toni took me to the chemist and got some medicine for me and had a talk to Mrs Jessie Rodgers, the promoter of Belle Vue. Because this was my first night there, they put me on last to give the medicine time to work a little. My head was still killing me. Toni said, 'Take it easy, and if you can't make it, pack it in.' I'd sooner die!

I got in the ring and my opponent cross-buttocked me and, as I landed, I thought my head had split in two. Was I in a state. The boy came in, took me in an arm-lock, which is a twisted arm, so that I was bent over, and then kicked me in the face. Shit – it was the best thing that could have happened. I was on the floor, thinking this is it, this is what Toni's been telling me about, this fellow is having a right go at me. All my pain went. I got up, smashed his face with my head, kneed him in the balls, kicked him when he was down and went down with him trying to bite his nose off. Of course I got disqualified. But I was in no pain any longer and no one was going to spread the word that I was easy meat. Jessie gave me lots of work after that, though Dick the Dormouse, her husband and our referee, warned me to behave in the ring. That gave Toni a laugh.

7

A Spooky Time

Although my career had really taken off, I always remained close to my family and saw them as often as I could. For no reason I could fathom, around this time my Mum and Dad suddenly started to attend spiritualist meetings. In fact, as time went on, they both became faith healers. When I first heard about it from them, I confess I thought they had gone round the bend. It was so out of character, particularly for my Dad who had always been the most down-to-earth sort of person. Frankly I just couldn't understand it. I used to tease them about it whenever I visited. 'How are the spooks going then?' I'd ask, and they'd both laugh with me, bless 'em. Little did I know I was soon going to laugh on the other side of my face.

It happened like this. One night in the gymnasium I was doing a very flashy 'Thieves Leap' over a wooden horse, which is just like going over a hurdle but that much higher. Over I went, high and fast but I landed on one foot instead of two. As soon as the first foot touched the floor I went to follow through and ran on and ouch! – over I went with the worst twisted ankle I can ever remember. There I was in agony on the floor, totally unable to get up. The boys had to carry me home. I couldn't put that foot to the floor and the pain was murder. It was so bad when I got home that I asked my wife to go and get Mum and Dad.

At that moment I was ready to try anything – even spooks! As soon as they arrived Mum went into her trance and started on my swollen ankle. She had been rubbing it gently for a couple of minutes before the pain became agonising. 'Stop,' I cried, 'that's all, no more, I've had enough.' I was jumping around the room on one leg. 'Blimey,' I yelled, 'that hurt.'

Mum looked at me and said quietly, 'It's all right, Joe – put your bad foot to the floor – it's OK now.' I did . . . and it was! Blimey, it was a miracle! I couldn't believe it. My ankle, I promise you, was all right – still swollen, but fine. 'Jump on it,' said Mum. I was dubious but this was my Mum speaking, so I jumped on it. It was lovely. I just couldn't take it in. I've had a few bad strains in my time and I know how long they take to heal and here I was – able to *jump* on it. I was thrilled – so much so that I thought 'I must find out what this is all about for myself', and I started sitting in on the healing sessions. I have to tell you – they work. I saw a friend of the family cured of a duodenal ulcer. Now it happens that I know what a duodenal ulcer is – because my poor old Dad had had one – and I know all about the pain it can give. I was in the circle that night the medium told this friend that he was almost cured, and again when he was told that he *was* cured. You have never seen such a happy, well man.

To be able to heal must be the most fulfilling feeling there is. As I said in a previous chapter, one of my bitterest regrets was not taking that Physiotherapy course offered to me when I was demobbed. I have always felt that with my strength and energy I might really have been able to heal people. Now here was another opportunity – and I loved every moment of my time spent in the healing circles.

But Mum was getting knocked out, she was giving so much to this work; I tell you the house was always full. One night I was there sitting in the circle: it's a nice room, a lovely big fire, beautiful flowers, about ten of us sitting quietly holding hands, eyes closed, relaxed – waiting for the medium to start her work – when who went out? ME! I was aware of something happening, but not sure what. The trouble was I didn't have any feeling of wanting to heal. I know I felt great power and strength; in fact, I was oozing this terrific energy. The mediums were trying to get whatever it was through but, so they told me afterwards, I was fighting them. Not that I knew anything about their efforts – I just felt this enormous power. How I wish I could have used that feeling to heal. I can't think of anything more wonderful.

Anyway, they brought me out of my trance and when they did I was freezing. I don't know where I had been – but it definitely wasn't hell – I was SO cold. I sat by the fire sobbing my heart out and for a long time I couldn't stop. And it wasn't over even when I had got myself under control.

At that time I lived in a top flat, eighty-four steps up past all the little porch entrances to the flats, and every night I was frightened out of my life. I used to take a deep breath and run up those stairs and wouldn't stop until I reached my flat, I was that scared. It was as if something had been freed in me and I was scared of meeting that 'thing' on the stairs. I should have had the sense to go to someone really experienced in Spiritualism and told them all about what had happened and how I felt. I am sure they could have explained and helped me, but I didn't go and I didn't go to any more meetings either. I was too frightened. Even to this day I sometimes get into my car and think there is someone else in there with me. At that time my hair used to stand on end and I'd look in the back to make sure I was alone. Anyway, one night I was wrestling in West Ham and Mrs Sammy King, the promoter's wife who used to run the canteen, spoke to me as I walked past to go to the dressing room. She asked me to see her before I left. After the match I got dressed and went to talk with her.

'Now Joe,' she said, 'do you know an elderly lady?' and she went on to describe my great grandmother (my Mum's grandmother) who was a beautiful Spanish lady. I told her who she was describing and then she described my grandfather on my father's side. It turned out she was a clairvoyant. She had no idea that I had dabbled in spiritualism, nor did she know anything else about me, apart from the fact that I used to make a great deal of money for her husband. But that night she told me that my great grandmother and grandfather were always with me, protecting me against harm. She said that I would always be safe because they were there all the time.

I felt so good that that night I got into the car and when I felt that scary feeling, I closed my eyes, relaxed and had this blissful feeling of total security. I still do that today if and when I get that crazy feeling. Now I don't know what you people out there think but I'm certain there is something in this spiritualism. Even now if I ever ask my Mum, who incidentally doesn't practise any more, to put her hands on me for any reason, I cry like a baby when she has finished. I don't want to, I try not to, I swear to myself beforehand that I will not – but I do every time. Makes you think – doesn't it?

8

King Of The Heavyweights

In the mid-1950s the uncrowned world-wide king of the wrestling heavyweights was Bert Assiratti. Ever since I started in the business I'd heard stories about him, about what a sadistic bastard he was and how much he loved to smash up his opponents. He had just come here from a long tour of India where he'd beaten all the champions, leaving a trail of blood right across the continent. But back in this country he could not get a fight. The reason was simple. When you know that from time to time you are going to come up against someone who is going to knock hell out of you, you just have to put up with it or pack up the game. But when that person quits the circuit for years the boys get used to working and not bleeding. So why should they start bleeding again just because Bert has decided to return? No one would go into the ring with him. I'd never met Bert, let alone fought him. So you can imagine how I felt when the phone rang in my flat and a voice said, 'Is that Joe Cornelius?'

'Yes.'

'This is Bert Assiratti, I've heard all about you.'

'Yes, and I've bloody heard all about you too.'

He burst out laughing. 'Will you fight me?'

'Yes, as long as you know, that I know, you're the guvnor.'

'Good, I'll come and meet you.'

I must have been mad after all I'd heard about him. But we met and it was arranged that I would challenge him at a local venue. The fight was a riot and Bert taught me the greatest lesson – before you beat a mug, make him look a champion. That's just what he did to me. He allowed me to knock him all over the place before he beat me – and even then he made it look a near thing.

I was running across the ring, hitting the ropes to give me momentum, jumping in the air and landing on his face with my feet – we call that a drop kick. Then I'd be back on my feet and off across the ring, hitting the ropes again and up into the air for another drop kick. I'd done this three or four times and was coming at him again when Bert ducked and I sailed over the top rope ten feet down to the floor. It's a wonder I didn't break my neck. I was face up and couldn't see where I was going. Of course I was counted out. The crowd went potty: everybody started rushing at the ring – Dad, brothers, cousins, friends, spectators – all trying to get at Bert, to kill him for what he had done to me. But what he had really done was to make me look a champion, and in the dressing room later, with everyone congratulating me, I really felt like one.

Bert put the seal on my status in the wrestling business. After that fight I started getting invitations from various European countries, saying that they had heard of me and asking if I would appear on certain dates. They never told me who I was to fight. But when I arrived it was always the same old story – there to meet me was dear Bert. The usual had happened – when Bert moved in the heavies moved out, and Bert had them send for me. He spread my fame for which I shall always be deeply grateful. I learnt a lot from Bert which stood me in good stead for twenty-odd years.

Injuries are an accepted part of the game and I've had my full share. It was the night before I was due to go to Paris that I went into the ring with that great black wrestler Ray Appollon. It was a good clean fight and we had the crowd on their feet, cheering us both. But right at the end Ray knocked the top of my collar bone. He picked me up and pile-drove me onto the floor, but my shoulder hit the deck first and took the brunt of the fall. So there I was with an arm I couldn't lift and a big fight in Paris the next day against a top heavyweight called Le Duke. I went to the doctor and made him write a letter in French explaining what injection I would need to get me into the ring. Next day I flew to Paris and handed the letter to the promoter. He was a worried man but he was grateful to me for not cancelling. We went to his home for a fabulous meal, on to his doctor and then to the venue, the Salva Gram, a building that reminded me of the Albert Hall. There I had my injection and watched the boys work. I had plenty of time because the top-of-the-bill bout was scheduled for about one o'clock in the morning.

This was my first time in France and I'd never seen top French wrestlers before. What fliers! They were in the air so much you'd think they had wings. They were more like trapeze artistes. I couldn't believe my eyes. I found the promoter and told him I didn't and couldn't work like that. It was crazy; it was not wrestling – it was aerobatics!

'Not to worry, Joe,' he said. 'Do your own work, everything will be OK.'

When it was time to go into the ring I couldn't feel my shoulder but I could lift my arm. I was well warmed up and determined to show the crowd what a good English boy could do. Out we came and everything was fine. We wrestled clean, clever and classic. The French loved it. We fought for sixty minutes and it was a draw. Right in the last round, Le Duke caught me on the chin and snapped my jaw to the ears. The pain was murder.

After the fight the promoter was so pleased with my performance he took me to his club for a steak. I couldn't touch it because I couldn't close my jaw. But I could drink and I downed my first-ever bottle of wine as if it were lemonade, I was so thirsty. By the time I'd drunk my fourth bottle without food, I started telling the promoter what bastards they all were – obviously it was time to go! He took me back to my hotel. There in the bar I met two Americans. Was I pleased to see them! It was as if I'd been away from home for years instead of hours. It was so good to talk English. We started drinking and they took me to a club. I don't remember being brought home. The next I knew was the hotel manageress shaking me, calling 'Monsieur, monsieur.' I woke up in a pool of red wine and I could hardly lift my head. I remember holding out a pile of money to the lady (come to think of it I probably paid for a new bed) and getting in a cab. No more, until I arrived at Waterloo and called on my old pal, Frank Duffy, who had a sports shop opposite the station.

'Frank, give me a painkiller.'

'Whatever is wrong with you?'

'Don't ask, give me something and phone the wife.'

I was still drunk, had a bad shoulder and an aching jaw. It was a long time before I could face wine again – and it still makes me drunk very quickly.

The next time I went to Paris I found myself staying in a hotel with an old mate, a very good English welter-weight. In the bar we met a charming 'business' lady. We had a few drinks, a few kisses and cuddles and went off fighting. After about a week of this, the lady made it clear that she fancied me, and poor Bill, who had been in France for a fortnight, still wasn't getting any nookie. Now, I'd never knowingly had a 'business' girl in my bed, so we made a deal with her. As she liked me so much, my mate would give her half her fee for the use of half her body and she and I could cuddle and kiss while Bill helped himself. It was quite a good arrangement and everybody was happy. *C'est la vie.*

9

On The Stage

It was Bobby Duranton who put me on the West End stage – though at the time all he wanted to do was put me on the floor. We were wrestling at Ghent in Belgium, when Bobby, a big muscle-man, tore my knee out of its socket and I had to leave the ring. The knee went back in time for me to fly the next day to Liverpool Stadium to fight Ray Hunter. In the first round I ran straight out of my corner and went to cross-buttock him, but my knee went out and I went down with Ray on top of me. I knew it was no good trying to carry on, so I threw in the towel. Billy Best, the promoter, wasn't at all pleased. Callous bastards, promoters. All they ever think about is time and money.

Back home the next day I got a message asking if I wanted to go into a show with Harry Secombe. I never knew exactly where the message came from, but I went down to the Prince of Wales Theatre, thinking the rest would do my knee good. There I met Lord Delfont and Harry.

'Well, Joe,' says Delfont, 'do you want to do a show with Harry and Beryl Reid at the London Palladium? It's a muscle sketch called "Males to Measure" in a revue called "Rocking the Town". All you have to do is walk out on the stage, flex your muscles and walk off.'

I told him, 'That's not me. I'm no muscle-man, I'm a wrestler and I've got a fair covering of flesh.'

They both laughed and asked me to strip off and show my chest. I did – and got the part.

I was very blasé about the whole thing because I was the big wrestler and quite famous by this time. This was to be just a short rest. Little did I know how long it would last and how much I would enjoy it.

We rehearsed at Harry's place in Chelsea with his wife Myra and his pianist Len Lighour. The story line was that Harry ran a shop selling husbands of all kinds, including lively French ones (Tony Mercer), rejects (Max Russell) and muscle-men (me). There were hilarious moments, like Beryl Reid bringing back a reject and Harry offering Tony or me in exchange. I used to whip into the spotlight in very brief briefs and then walk down to the front of the stage. It always made the audience sit up. Harry came with Beryl to the centre front of me and said, 'How about that?'

Beryl replied, 'Is he real?'

But what the audience never heard was what Beryl said in a whisper to Harry: 'What a small cock he's got!'

I always had a job to stop myself laughing. One night I thought I'd have my own back. I stuffed three face flannels down my briefs, but it was too much. They stuck out like a third leg. I was going to take one out when suddenly my cue came and I had to whip into the spotlight with this bulge in front of me. When Beryl saw it she nearly fell off her chair. Harry gave me an odd look and walked down to the front. By this time I was killing myself laughing. I struck up a pose and Beryl whispered to Harry, 'That's definitely a prop.'

Harry and Beryl went into hysterics. I collapsed and started to walk off, I was so helpless with laughter. Harry pulled me back and steered us through the sketch. I don't think the audience knew for sure what we were laughing at but, because belly laughing is so infectious, they were in hysterics too. It went on for what seemed ages – a wonderful night. When I came off the stage I got a good telling-off from the stage manager. 'What are you trying to do – shut us down?' he yelled.

Working with Harry Secombe was great. It was a laugh a minute. We were on stage one night, doing the finale of the 'Top Graders', in which we used to run backwards and forwards across the stage passing each other. Suddenly Harry hid from me behind the 'tabs' and as I'm running back I'm wondering where the hell he is.

I couldn't see him but I knew he would be out to barge into me if he got the chance. Now Harry wasn't any lightweight, and if we connected and I wasn't ready I knew he could wind up in the orchestra pit. Anyway, there I was running along when suddenly there he was – charging straight at me. I just had time to dive off into the tabs as he crashed into me, knocking the stagehand behind the tabs flying. It brought the house down!

After the show Harry said 'Let's keep that in, Joe', so every night we did it, and every night I had to keep a very sharp eye on him because he was always trying to catch me unawares and send ME flying. He is a really great man – they threw the mould away after making him.

I had many good times at the Palladium – a wonderful place for pulling birds. One night Tom, a pal of mine, brought a girl with him to meet me at the stage door and discuss a date we planned for that evening. 'You can go up to my dressing room,' I said. It was okay with the stage door keeper, and I could trust him. So up Tom went with the bird. When I came off stage later, I found my dressing room was locked and I guessed that dirty sod was having a screw. So I ran onto a small flat roof that looked right into my room and there was the dear Tom, fucking away like a good'un. In no time a crowd of stage hands had joined me to watch the cabaret. When Tom realised we were watching he decided to do a bit of showmanship for us, and when I saw his arse going fifteen to the dozen I thought it was time I got in on the act – but he wouldn't let me into my room. I had to start bashing the door down before he would open it. The boys behind me all came in – and what a party we had. I always had plenty of drink in my room. The only trouble was that there were no stage hands around to shift any scenery – most of them were in my room. The party wound up with Tom going mad (as he did in those days) because he thought someone had pinched his bird. What had really happened was that we heard Jack, the stage manager, coming to see what the hell his crew were up to. So one of the George Mitchell Singers took Tom's girl down the back staircase and out of the building. Tom didn't believe our story and started to run amok with a knife. I was the only one who could calm him down.

There have been only two occasions in my life when I had a nickname. In the army at Dover I was called Darkie and at the Palladium the dancing boys called me 'Whinnie the Whale'. I'll tell you how it came about. In those days of 'Rocking the Town', there were no baths or showers in the dressing rooms, and because I had to have body make-up along with the dancing boys, they put a portable shower in the boys' dressing room. When the show ended I used to go to their room to shower. They were very quiet and subdued at first, not knowing me, an outsider to showbusiness and a wrestler. It wasn't until they realised I knew the gay scene, and didn't mind them at all, that they relaxed. So much so that, while I was in the shower, they used to try and touch me up. They called me Whinnie the Whale because of the mess I made with the water. They were always pummelling me in the guts in fun because they envied my muscles – but there was one boy who went too far. I knew what he was after, and one night, when he became far too fresh with me at the stage door, I gave him one in the belly he wouldn't forget for a while. Needless to say I never had any more trouble with him.

While I was at the Palladium, I was taking out one of the dancing girls. She was in a sketch in which she had to kiss one of the gay boys. I often wondered whose cock had been in his mouth, and she had strict instructions from me to turn her cheek and not her lips to him. All the time I was at the Palladium, I still did my Saturday night in the print, on the *Observer*. I'd finish the matinée and go straight to work with my make-up on. You can imagine the catcalls I got, but the boys got used to it in the end and when I had to go back to the Palladium for the last performance they covered for me.

We had a great FOC (Father of the Chapel) called Harry Groatrex who held that office for thirty-five years. He was a stern, understanding, snuff-taking gentleman. He knew everything that went on and when to turn a blind eye. One day Bill Cash, the boss, said to Harry, 'Is that Cornelius in tonight?'

Harry replied, 'Yes, Bill, he's about somewhere.'

'That's funny,' said Bill, 'I've just seen him at the Palladium.'

He'd been to the matinée of course. All my mates were very good to me and appreciated that no matter what antics I got up to, I knew my work and did it well. After all I belonged to a printing family.

At the end of our Palladium run, ITV threw a party on stage. I was having a great time when a chap came up to me and started talking about the show and about wrestling. He told me he did judo and then leant closer and whispered, 'Can I take you home?' I had to laugh, I mean – I hardly looked the part.

Anyway, I told him I had my own car 'thank you'. Saucy bastard – he made me feel like a tart.

After the party, pissed as a pudding, I pinched a big gâteau to take home to the wife. I got into my car and tipped the whole thing all over me. I tried rubbing the cream off with a cloth but I guess I didn't do a very good job and I looked a right state when I got in. I told the wife about the accident with the cake – God knows what she really thought I'd been up to – but she put me to bed just the same. The closing of the show was heartbreaking for me. I didn't get any telegrams on the first night but I certainly got them at the end, and knew what they meant. I was drunk for three days. I couldn't bear the thought of not being with all those lovely people I'd lived with for nine months. It was like losing a great big happy family.

10

On Tour With Lily

I have always had a hankering for the buying and selling game and while I was at the Palladium I started to dabble again. I did it for fun really, not profit. I found jars of caviar for two shillings and sold them for five. I just turned my money over, and the stars were good buyers. Then I made a bad mistake and went overboard buying bent gear. It was all set up for me and I bought a load of lovely dresses on the cheap, all boxed. The boys who were flogging them wanted to take them out of the boxes but I said 'No, I want the boxes, they'll sell easier.' So I loaded up, took them home and was doing a return trip for the rest when I saw the law all over the street. So I scarpered. When I got home I sent the wife and kids round to my mother's. Then I went on the missing list, not knowing how easy it is to get bail and get out of the nick. I figured I'd work the Friday and Saturday shows and then give myself up, and maybe I'd have enough time over the weekend to get out of the police station and back to the Palladium for the Monday matinée.

But on Saturday, as I was doing 'Males to Measure' with Harry and Beryl in the matinée, I saw the police in the wings. I nearly shit myself. As soon as I came off stage the stage manager said, 'You've got someone to see you in your dressing room.' Up I went and there was Sandy, a smashing police sergeant, another CID man and a uniformed officer. The uniformed officer took out his truncheon and I started to laugh. I was so glad to get it over.

'We won't need this, will we Joe?' Sandy smiled.

'I hope not,' I said. 'Please put it away, Constable.'

Then I asked them to let me do the evening show, and they agreed. They were really good and fair to me because, as Sandy told me later, they didn't think I was really a criminal – just bloody stupid.

On the way home we stopped at a pub and had a drink while I told them my story. When we arrived at my house in Bermondsey there were just the four of us, no one else in sight. But when I opened the door it was like Ali Baba and his forty thieves, except they were all police. They came from everywhere – God knows where they had been hiding – and they went all over the house. I had some very good (but very dodgy) brandy. So I asked them if they wanted a drink. They did – and I poured it out in half-pint glasses. I couldn't get rid of it quick enough.

Opposite me lived a little old man whom I used to look after. I told the coppers I'd like to take a drink over to him in case I never got back. 'Sure,' said Sandy. I took over a couple of bottles of brandy, some coffee and odds and ends, and kidded the old man I was going on holiday for a while. Then the police took me to the station, did the fingerprints and took the pictures and sent me home again. Of course they found a load of cloth in my garage, as well as the dresses in my house. I said that I'd let the garage to one of the boys in the market. Naturally, they wanted his name, which I never gave (there was a strict code then, not like now). They said that if I told them who owned the cloth in the garage, I could probably get off with the dresses, which I'd told them were bought as out-of-season stock. But I wouldn't reveal the name, and having two lots of stolen goods was too much of a coincidence, so I got charged with both.

The preparations for the case went on for six months and nearly drove me mad. Before it was heard, the show at the Palladium had ended and the thought of having to go to prison put me into a terrible state. The boys I used to knock about with dropped me like a hot brick, which was the best thing that ever happened to me because I'm the loyal type, and if they had helped me at that time I'd have been in the game for good. But the thought of being locked up frightened me to death and I went on the drink. I have always rebelled against anything that restricts me. Now I no longer cared if my wife knew I was larking about with girls. I'd come home with lipstick over my shirt or stay out all night.

When the case came on I had a great barrister. Imagine the scene in court with all the dresses and cloth laid out. The prosecution went on and on about the stolen goods, but when they'd finished my barrister said quietly, 'I don't think we have to go any further. We don't know that this cloth has ever been stolen.'

It was a point of law but I said to myself 'Blimey, you're going a bit strong here, there's all this gear spread out and you're saying it's not stolen. It's crazy.' But the case about the cloth was thrown out of court, leaving only the case about the dresses. I had arranged for a very big dress manufacturer, who was also a wrestler, to be in court and vouch that out-of-season dresses could be bought very cheaply, and that the price I had paid would have been about right. Of course, he was my pal, but what he said was true. At least, I believed him!

My barrister said to the Judge, 'My client has been a mug. He's been an idiot to deal with people who sold him the goods. He is a good working boy, he's always had a good job but he's made a big mistake. I suggest to the jury that they bring in a verdict of not guilty.'

They did – the best thing that ever happened to me. I ran out of the court and vowed 'Never again.'

Just after the case finished, 'Rocking the Town' was due to go on tour. I apologised to my wife for being such an idiot and asked her forgiveness, which she readily gave, and when the tour started I sent all my money home until I'd paid off my debts.

The tour began in Newcastle with Harry, Ann Lancaster taking Beryl's place, the Gimma Boys, an adagio act, Rudy Horn with his great juggling, the Monkees and the girls and boys of the chorus. It was a wonderful show that packed them in no matter where we went.

That first week I had a stage manager who was a right bully to the chorus. He would literally pull them out of their dressing rooms and shout at them. This went on for days before Harry gave an after-show party on the stage. The finale steps, on which the girls and boys of the chorus used to stand while all the stars were accepting their bows, were still there. During the party we all did the conga along the top of these steps while the pianist played for us. Suddenly the stage manager ran out to the front.

'Get off those steps,' he yelled, 'and stop this party.'

With that I'd had enough. I jumped from the top of the steps and landed right at his feet.

'Cunt,' I yelled at the top of my voice. 'Who do you think you are?' With that he disappeared.

Harry, like the gentleman he was, said, 'Come on, let's forget about it and all enjoy ourselves,' and we had a smashing party without the stage manager.

The next morning I met him in the wardrobe. 'Sorry about last night, Joe,' he said, meaning 'You've only got to say a nice word to me and I'm yours.'

'That's all right,' I said, 'we shouldn't have been on your steps.'

'But I'm not afraid of you,' he said aggressively.

'You cunt,' I said, 'I'll kill you!'

And he was gone again. After that, if any of the boys or girls wanted anything in that show, they came to me and I arranged it.

It was a strange period of my life. I'd always wanted to be the good fellow and I always tried to be nice and help people. I wanted to be liked but, because of the court case over the dresses and cloth, I realised that it doesn't matter how nice you are: some people like you and some hate you, no matter what. So now I didn't care a sod about anybody. If anyone said a word wrong, I'd go for them, whereas before I'd let people do and say anything. I liked the power I had over people because they wanted to be my friend rather than my enemy. How can a man get to be so mixed up? Thank God I got myself sorted out later.

The tour took us to many towns and we always played the No. 1 theatres. I used to love the train calls when all the company would meet at the station, take over most of the train and go to the next town and start looking for digs.

But at the start I was green. For a try-out before Newcastle, I arrived by car in Birmingham and said to the stage door keeper, 'What hotel am I staying at?'

'Don't you know?' he said.

'Come on, don't mess about, where am I?'

'Sorry, sir, you find your own digs.'

What a let-down! Me, Joe Cornelius, the big wrestling star, with no hotel. Just then, a couple of girls from the chorus came along.

'You looking for digs?'

'Yes.'

'You can come with us if you like.'

And they took me to their digs to see if I could get in. What an eye-opener! We paid about £3.50 a week, food and board. Blimey! No wonder some of the kids starved for the art. But I loved it, and it was like a party every night.

* * *

During the tour my knee started going out again. To start with it wasn't anything to worry about. I'd just bend my leg, putting my hand against the knee joint, straighten the leg and back the knee would go. Until the night when the bloody thing got stuck. I could not get the cartilage back, no way – not even when I got the boys pulling so hard it's a wonder they didn't wrench the leg out of the socket. There was one sketch in which I had to do a couple of dance steps on my heels, and that made me sweat with agony. When the knee was in a bent position there was no pain, but to go back on my heels I had to straighten the knee. Was I glad when that sketch was over! Eventually, the knee went back, but I realised it wouldn't be right again until I'd had an operation.

But I had Lily to take my mind off it. She was in the show and we first met in Newcastle. I discovered that she'd never had an orgasm. What a challenge! We went to a friend's flat and we lay in each other's arms and I didn't rush anything, just caressed her very gently and didn't attempt to touch her vital parts until she was crying out for it. I kissed and stroked her from head to toe, inside and out; I didn't leave a crevice untouched by my tongue. I hadn't touched her with my hands or cock yet, but when I did, she wanted it bad, and it happened. She came, blimey did she come! She screamed out so much it frightened me. I think all those years of saving it up exploded at once. She was so happy and so was I.

We spent a lot of time together after that and had many, many lovely sexy days and nights. I remember one night she could hardly walk, she'd come so much.

And another time, the stage director caught us doing it on the stage. He said, 'I can't shift a bit of scenery without finding you two fucking behind it.' In the dressing room Lily would sit on the dressing table, lights all around it, and I'd sit on the chair, just eating her up. It was a very mutual arrangement. I remember in Manchester thinking what else we could do, position-wise. Now, she wasn't a small girl, but I lifted her up by her bum. She was sitting on my hands, when I lifted her up into the air and then lowered her on my face. It was fortunate that I had an 18½″ neck. It wasn't very comfortable, but who else had kissed a clitoris like this before? We had her clitoris so sensitive that I just used to put my finger-pad lightly on it and it would jump all over the place. She could never control it and would come time and time again.

When we got to Birmingham a big crowd of us found digs in a great house in Hagley Road. The lady was an old theatre pro and ran the house just for show people. One night after the show, Lily and I had our dinner and went up to our large room. On the way up I noticed the candelabras with the most beautiful candles in them. 'Why not?' I thought. So I took the candles with me. Why not have a little help? So we started making love as usual and I brought the candles into play. It was quite successful because now I could fill all the holes at once, one in the pussy, one in the arse and my cock in her mouth. It was lovely. Lily loved it too.

After the tour was over we all went our own ways. Lily and I saw each other a few times. It was always nice. Thanks for wonderful memories, Lily, I'll always treasure those good times together. And it wasn't just the sex – although we certainly did have some!

11

On My Knees

After the tour I had the chance to go into another Palladium show which would have taken me out of town again. But when I told my wife about it she accused me of wanting to go with the show girls. She was probably right! So I picked up the telephone and called Delfont. 'Bernie,' I said, 'I won't be there.'

'What do you mean?'

'Don't ask me mate, it's domestic.'

And that was the end of my theatre career.

So it was back to wrestling. With all that showbiz experience behind me I reckoned I ought to make more of a show of myself for my return to the ring. I went to St John Roper, who dressed the Palladium shows, and told him what I wanted. He made me two of the most beautiful, full length gold lamé cloaks, metallic elastic tunics and silver boots. The promoters loved the gear and billed me as The Dazzler.

When I fought at the small baths where the crowds are right on top of you, they would keep hollering at me 'When are you gonna dazzle us, Joe?' And I'd tell them that when the cloak came off the dazzle was over. But I did dazzle them a good few times before my old injury came back and I had to go into the ring with a bandaged knee. And worse was to come. I fought Gordon Nelson, and he tore my other knee cartilage and a ligament. I now had two dodgy legs and it was crazy! How can a dazzler have both his knees strapped up?

At one time I wasn't off crutches for more than three weeks on the trot, and I had a few spells in hospital. My first visit was to the Middlesex, where the surgeon said, 'Joe, if you will do me a favour and let my student examine your knee, I'll have you in this afternoon and do the job tomorrow.'

I told him, 'You've got a deal,' and I whipped off to the promoters to tell them to cancel my bout. Cold-blooded sods that they are, they just said, 'Must you really cancel?' and put their heads back into the books trying to find a substitute for me. They didn't even say goodbye, kiss my arse or anything. Real caring folk!

The next day I was lying on the bed in the operating theatre while the surgeon talked to his pupils. He called one or two out to examine my leg to find out what was wrong with it. It was hard for them really because, although I could put my knee out and back with no trouble, I had kept my legs in good muscular condition and nothing showed. After one of the students had finished his examination and had announced that he couldn't find anything wrong, the surgeon said, 'Have you got anything to say, Joe?'

I said, 'I don't know what kind of surgeon this man will make, but I know he'll make a great lover, he's so gentle.'

The whole theatre broke down, the catcalls were hilarious and the poor fellow blushed deep red.

Years later I was in St Thomas's waiting for my eyes to be stitched up when the doctor said, 'You don't know me, but I'm called "the lover" thanks to you – do you remember? Ever since that day in the Middlesex Hospital it's been my nickname.'

As he spoke he was making a big thing out of threading the needle, but he was still a very gentle man and did a nice job on my eyes.

I had to stay in the Middlesex after they'd fixed my knee and that was the first time I'd ever had to use a bedpan. I had to support myself by holding onto a chain, but I wound up climbing up the chain to get away from the stuff. I was mad with embarrassment and swearing something terrible. The nurses came and got me down, cleaned me up and told me not to worry. But the next time I wanted to go I waited until all the nurses were out of the way, got out of my bed and hopped down the corridor to the lavatories. I got into a lot of trouble, but there was no way I was going through all that climbing up the chain business again.

What I liked best about the Middlesex was the little nurses rubbing my bum with spirit so that I wouldn't get bed sores. I asked them to do it so often that I came out with a pickled bum!

* * *

But that wasn't the end of my knee trouble. I finished up having both cartilages removed and then, as a last resort, went to Camden Rehabilitation Centre, which specialised in getting people with normal injuries back to work. When I arrived they reckoned they had a challenge. They knew who I was and they worked on me for three months as if I were a world champion. Came the day when they took me to a running track which was on a slope – and I held back. When you are running downhill it is more of a strain on your joints and I was afraid that I wouldn't be able to stand the pain and the crunching if the knees went out and I fell to the ground in agony. But my instructor, bless him, said, 'Joe, if the knee is going to go you are in the right place for it to be sorted out, so come on, grit your teeth and go – shit or bust!' I thought sod it, I don't care, and I went. I screamed and I ran as fast as I could. I ran like the wind down the track and up the track – and my knees were okay. I could have cried with pleasure. I can't thank Camden Rehabilitation Centre enough, they saved my legs and saved my wrestling career.

When I got home I said to my wife, 'That's it. If my knees go again I'm finished with wrestling. I've got to stand on these all my life.' So I bound my knees up and went back to the ring. I had been out of the game for quite a while and the other fighters expected me to go carefully. My first fight was with Bill Verner, a nice boy weighing about twenty stone, but he could be a little rough if he was allowed. He had taken a few beltings in India and was in the mood to give some himself. When I arrived I went to a room by myself and started to skip. I was determined to have my body ready. I skipped and skipped until I got my blood boiling. When we entered the ring Bill expected me to come out like a cripple. Instead, I flew around his head like a moth. I don't think I'd ever been so fit in my life. Bill didn't know what had hit him and from that day on my knees have been fine. I still look after them and no one is allowed to go near them, let alone touch them.

After that first outing I knew my knees were okay but, to give them added support, I strapped both of them up with six-inch elastic bandages, put knee straps over them and, as you can't have a baby-faced wrestler with bandaged legs, I decided to wear tights. So I abandoned the spangled trunks and the silver boots and went into black tights and trunks. In the beginning it wasn't easy to convince the public that a boy in tights is a baby face, because normally tights on a man mean he is a villain. But with hard work and clean wrestling I kept the name of Dazzler all through the rest of my wrestling career.

12

I Fight Carnera

In the wrestling game you have so many fights you get blasé about who you're working with on any particular night. What does it matter? You go in the ring, same as you have done for the last five nights, and take it in your stride. The only thing that might make the adrenalin run would be to find yourself on with somebody special. There weren't many of them, but I'll tell you about a few.

I went to Bath, got off the train and strolled down to the hall, not a care in the world, a confident happy soul. But when I got to the hall I saw a poster announcing the appearance of 'Primo Carnera'. I was impressed! And the old adrenalin was running. In fact it was ruddy well galloping!

'Christ!' I thought, 'am I really going to fight the one and only Primo Carnera?' I couldn't get into the dressing room fast enough. And there he was – a giant of a man.

The world's heavyweight boxing champion, vast and impressive, just like all the pictures I'd seen of him. The promoters, who should have warned me, introduced us. Primo came over to me with a smile. I must have looked like a small boy to him. I put out my hand, saying how proud I was to be fighting him.

'Nice to meet you, boy,' he said. Then he took my outstretched thumb with his huge hand and started to wank it! What a man! He was letting me know he was one of the chaps. What a relief!

He wasn't just an ex-world champion, nor just the biggest thing you've ever seen, he was humorous, kind and a gent. When we met in the ring and came to the middle for instructions I figured he was so big that I only had one chance and that was to keep flying. Running across the ring, using the ropes for speed, tackling him, drop-kicking, anything to stop him getting those hands on me. He stood up and struck a boxing pose and I thought 'Blow me – if he hits me with one of those fists, I'm finished.' He did and I was.

The fight lasted three rounds, with Primo standing waiting for me while I buzzed round his head like a fly. And then he nailed me. Wham! I was proud to be knocked out by such a man – the one and only Primo Carnera.

At Belle Vue, Manchester, I was billed one night with the infamous, bearded, Bill Benny – a right villain, weighing about eighteen stone. When I got to the dressing room I saw that poor Bill had got one whole leg pressure-bandaged. Mrs Jessie Rodgers, the promoter, didn't want to cancel the bout and pleaded with Bill to carry on. As most of his work consisted of punching and wrestling dirty, a leg in a bandage didn't matter much to him. Bill was a great showman and nothing worried him, least of all a bad leg. The bell sounded and I came out of my corner in a flying roll which brought me right to his corner. As he turned around I grabbed an arm lever and he grabbed my hair and pulled me over the ropes on to the apron of the ring and kicked me, with his good leg, out of the ring. I jumped back into his corner and we swapped holds. He was swearing at the crowd and making all the dirty moves, but so far he hadn't ventured out of his corner. The fight went marvellously, considering the fact that we wrestled in his corner for three rounds. I got an arm-lock on him again and he shouted out to the crowd, 'Is this all he knows?' pointing at the arm-lock. The saucy bastard! I'd wrestled him in his corner for three rounds to save his leg and now he was having a right go at me. So with that, I monkey-climbed him, jumping up with my feet on his thighs, my hand round his neck, falling back and whipping him with my feet, sending him sailing through the air. But where I would normally have put him on his back, I gave a last-second push with my hands, which brings a man on his feet. Served him right! He screamed. I ran over and did the monkey-climb again, shooting him through the air to land, all eighteen stone of him, on his bad leg. Of course, the fight was over. It's a pity one has to resort to this sort of behaviour, but if I'd let him get away with taking a liberty with me, others would have tried. As it happened, after that the word went round and made the boys a bit more cautious of me. I was definitely not just a pretty face!

My match with Billy Two-Rivers was on television and quite a few viewers still remember it. Nowadays Billy is a delegate for the Canadian Red Indians and this year he was a member of the delegation that applied to the British Government for help in their cause. Billy has a good brain and a great sense of humour. I shall never forget giving him his first fight in this country. It was a Relwisko promotion.

George Relwisko had a talk with me about this Red Indian who had just come in. I was an established 'baby face' and Billy should have been on with a villain so that he could show off his war dance before he did his dreaded 'chop'. His speciality was this very effective chop to the throat or chest that usually finished the bout. The promoter said, 'Joe, we want to build this fellow up in this country and the people want to see his war dance, so see what you can do.'

Now, my kind of work didn't call for Billy's kind of reprisal, but business is business. When we entered the ring Billy was wearing the most fantastic chieftain's headdress and he looked out of this world. We went to our corners, off came the headdress and the fight began. Out I came, very wary, because if he could fight as well as he could wear that headdress I was in for a very exciting match. We sized each other up for a couple of rounds, not doing anything special. I was just doing my clean, clever stuff and he was just wrestling. So I thought it was time to liven things up, as I often did after some straight wrestling. As we came together again, I put the most beautiful elbow into his neck. You should have seen his face change. Sparks started to fly from his eyes. I picked him up off the floor and slammed him down. Up he jumped. The crowd were waiting for his war dance but he couldn't do it because I had taken him back into a head-lock and down to the floor. The timing for the dance was not right yet. Another couple of rounds and I could feel the crowds were really getting restless. I hit him with a right elbow, picked him off the floor, whacked him again and down he went, and I grabbed him down there. The crowd jumped up and so did Billy and started his war dance. The crowd were going crazy, they had never seen anything like it before – and neither had I.

I jumped out of the ring and stood on the apron to watch. With that, Billy grabbed my head and pulled me over the top rope back into the ring. The crowd had forgotten all about me being so nice and now they wanted Billy to kill me. So I went mad and, as he came in, I stuck a fist into his belly and as he turned over I kicked him in the face. I was back to my street-fighting days, but he jumped up and was back on the reservation, dancing all over the place, frightening me to death. He whipped me into the ropes and – chop! – down I went. He picked me up, which is not allowed, but no one cared. He threw me into the ropes again and – chop! – that was the end of me. I was on the floor, counted out, and Billy Two-Rivers was still war-dancing like mad. The entire crowd were on their feet, screaming, shouting and going crazy. Billy was their God. The Red man had triumphed. Only in England could it have happened.

I got a good pay-packet, Billy got his war dance, the

promoters got a packed house, everybody was happy. After all, I could always come back next week and win the crowd back again.

When I was working at Belle Vue, I used to catch the train that got me to Manchester in time to go dancing before the match. A few dances would loosen me up from the train journey and get me ready for the fight. One evening, while I was dancing, I saw a very pretty girl, demure and conservatively dressed. I asked her to dance and then invited her to come to Belle Vue to watch me wrestle. She did, and we met afterwards and went dancing again. She was quiet and shy but agreed to come to my hotel. There she turned from this quiet little girl to a raving sex maniac. I don't think, up to that time, that I'd ever had a girl who was so sexy. And a peculiar thing about her was that when she climaxed it shot out just like a man's – not once but continually. By the time we left the hotel I was highly embarrassed and could never go back to it again because we left the bed in such a state. We saw each other a few times after that, but I had to laugh when I heard that one of my wrestling pals had pinched her, taken her to his home while his wife was away and made love to her on a sheepskin rug. Can you imagine! The girl was coming all over the place and matting up that sheepskin rug something terrible. He had to do a high-speed cleaning job before his wife came back. Served him right!

Speaking of high speed cleaners, someone should certainly have sent Jack Pye for the treatment because Jack Pye was the dirtiest fighter there ever was; yet somehow there was something about him that the crowds loved. We looked quite alike with our dark wavy hair and plenty of Brylcreem. We both wore black tights, but he was a villain and I was a baby face, he was fifty and I was twenty-five, he weighed sixteen-and-a-half stone and I weighed fourteen stone. In one of the first fights we had at Belle Vue, he was kicking and punching me all over the place, and was disqualified. I was on the floor as he went out of the ring and walked away. I got up and dived over the top rope and landed right on top of him, ten feet down. I hadn't been there a minute when the crowd took over. It's one thing when a big villain wrestler is walking towards and past you, giving you a threatening look in the eye, and quite another when he is on the floor, flat as a pancake. The crowd kicked him to pieces until the promoter, Jessie Rodgers, who was quite a big girl, and the ref, Dick the Dormouse, her husband, rescued him and got him to the dressing room. Was I told off!

'Do whatever you like to the villain in the ring, but never stop him outside the ring,' Jessie said.

Jack called me a silly young bastard, but he forgave me and we went on to have some fantastic bouts over the years.

Mike Mareno was a general in the ring. He's dead now, bless him, but he taught me a hell of a lot. Once at Pershal Hall in Hagley Road, Birmingham – a small, compact place where the punters were right on top of you – I kneed Mike right in the face. I nearly caved his head in. Eventually, he got up off the canvas and said, 'Come here, I'll show you how to do it without caving a head in.'

He then proceeded to give me a lesson on throwing a knee. The crowd hadn't got a clue what was going on; they didn't know he was teaching me in their time. Years later, at Shoreditch, the crowd had the needle to Mike. When we started to wrestle they had a right go at him. I took him into a head-lock and he just lay there. The crowd started to slow-handclap. Mike still lay there and said to me, 'Do you mind, Joe?'

I replied, 'No, be my guest.' It is vital never to let the crowd dictate what is going to happen in the ring. We had the 'Richard' (raspberries and booing) for five rounds, and Mike just wouldn't do a thing. The promoter was quite angry when we came off.

'What the bloody hell was that all about?'

Mike told him that no crowd was going to dictate to him.

'But you had the "Richard" for five rounds.'

'Yes, but they had what we wanted to give, didn't they?' What could the promoter say?

The next week I was back there with Al Hayes. 'We might have some heat against me, Al,' I told him. We came out of our corners. I took Al in a head-lock and put him to the ground. The crowd shouted, 'Turn it up, Joe, we saw all that last week!' I stayed with the head-lock for a while. The crowd went very quiet – no 'Richard', no catcalls – they'd learnt their lesson. So I gave them what they really wanted and were they pleased! We had a blinding contest. It was just another lesson that I had learned from Mike Mareno.

I still see my old pal Johnny Peters at least once a week. When he and I decided to wrestle tag together (that means four in the ring) I said to Johnny, 'You're the local boy, you be captain.' Brighton was Johnny's town and we were a great hit there. Sometimes we had two boxes of royalty coming to watch us. We had such a following that the police asked to be told when we were working in Brighton so that they could divert the traffic. I would get Johnny to do most of the work. He'd be wrestling and go to tag and I'd say, 'You're the captain, you do the work.' Poor Johnny was quite breathless at times.

I wanted to go to live in Brighton but Johnny would not hear of it. 'There's only room for one of us here, you stay out,' he said. How we both regret that decision. In our heyday, we could have opened any business in that town and made a mint. I live near Brighton now, at the Five Bells public house, Chailey, so we still see each other and reminisce about the good old days when we were The Dynamic Duo instead of the old bastards we are today.

One of many crazy nights that neither of us will ever forget, was the time Johnny got badly cut. We were tagging against Bruno Elrington and Danny Lynch, a wicked pair of fighters, when Danny split Johnny's head with a chair. Poor Johnny needed sixteen stitches in it. The crowd were furious. They invaded the ring and Bruno and Danny were fighting for their lives.

Johnny said, 'Let's go and help them.'

'Fuck them!' I said. 'They asked for it, let the crowd have them.'

The police had to rescue them and get them out of the ring. Johnny was put on a stretcher to be taken to hospital and be stitched up, and while he was lying there I got my thumb up his arse. He was trying not to show the pain he was in and I was killing myself laughing. Why did I do those things? God knows.

Internationally I was known as The Thumb Man and The Pisser. It had begun when I was fighting a Frenchman in Shoreditch. The French were very fit, flashy types. I didn't like them much then and I'm not too keen on them now. If they had the chance they would pinch the whole show and try to make you look useless. My work was always clean, clever and classic but this particular Frenchman was flying all over the ring trying to look wonderful and make a name for himself. But I was on my toby (ground) and he was trying to make me look silly by not giving me any of the show. So I got behind him, brought him down to the floor and goosed him, thumb up his arse. He could not get away from me, and started to sweat. He couldn't very well tell the Shoreditch crowd in French that I'd got my thumb up his arse, they wouldn't have understood. Now, I don't know if you've ever had a thumb up your arse but, I promise you, it slows you down. When I eventually let him up, he was like a baby and we gave the crowd a good match. And that's how my speciality thumb-hold started.

13

The Zebra Kid

He was an American. He weighed twenty-four stone and wore a mask and a costume striped like a zebra. So they called him The Zebra Kid. But to me he was always George. I never knew his surname. A college Catch-As-Catch-Can Wrestling champion, he could skip and play handball like a lightweight. We were natural opposites, George being so ugly in his mask and me a pretty boy – well, pretty by wrestling standards. We had some fantastic matches with the crowds screaming for me to kill him and take his mask off for what he had done to me, like punching and wrestling dirty. But we were good pals out of the ring and that's why I tried to help him when he hit bad times. George had been wrestling in Greece. When he came back he had no money and couldn't get much work. He blamed the English promoters but wouldn't say why. He wanted to lose weight and put himself on sleeping pills, reckoning that the more he slept, the less he would eat. He was in a bad mental state.

One Sunday morning I was in the Jermyn Street Turkish baths when I had a telephone call from my wife saying, 'Please get to the Zebra, he's going to shoot himself.'

I had soap all over me at the time and I didn't even stop to dry myself. I half dressed in the car and went straight to Streatham to the Zebra's flat. There he was in bed – with a gun in his hand!

I said, 'What the fuck do you think you're doing, George?'

'I've had enough of those bastard promoters,' he snarled. 'They've had all my money and I'm going to end it all.'

'Don't be a dope, George,' I said. 'Don't give in to them, they'd like you to do just that. Come on, let's have some tea.'

'You cock-sucking limey,' he snapped, 'all you ever think about is tea.'

I knew then that we stood a good chance of saving him because he loved having a verbal go at me. I was silent for a moment, then I said, 'I tell you what, mate, let your wife and kids go over to my place and I'll stay with you and we'll sort this out.'

'Okay, you old cock-sucker' (it was his favourite expression) – but he still had the gun and wouldn't let it go.

'Now look, George,' I pleaded, 'you may have done your money but you'll get it back again. What's money anyway?'

'Those bastards have double-crossed me. If it wasn't for them I'd be all right and now they're giving me the treatment so that I can't get any work.'

'Don't be crazy, you know you're one of the best. You can get work anywhere. Go to Germany, Kizer (a big German promoter) would love to have you.'

'Fuck them, I've had enough.'

By this time the tea had come and his wife left with mine to go home. I knew I had to keep trying to persuade the Zebra to live and fight it out with the promoters. I talked and talked and talked.

'Close your goddam mouth for Chrissake, you're giving me a headache,' he said, which wasn't bad for someone who sixty minutes earlier was going to shoot himself. He was still in bed and I had my arm around his shoulders. Just when I thought I was winning him over he pointed the gun at his foot and started to squeeze the trigger. I didn't look forward to seeing his foot splattering all over the wall, but I reckoned that once he'd done it he would let go of the gun and I'd be able to grab it. At least I could save his life, if not his foot. His finger tightened on the trigger. I screwed up my eyes for the explosion and – it clicked on an empty chamber. He laughed.

'You bastard,' I said, 'you've been fooling me all this time.'

'Oh no I ain't,' said George and reached under the pillow, grabbed a clip of bullets, lumbered out of the bed and put a bullet in the chamber. By this time I was on my feet, not knowing what the hell to expect.

'I've had enough of your goddam talking,' he said – and aimed the gun at me.

I was so scared I could hardly speak. All I could think of saying was, 'Now you've made me mad, George, I'm going to finish with you.'

And he put the gun down and said, 'You've given

me a headache again.' After that he seemed almost normal.

'Let me go to sleep, I'm okay now,' he said.

'You sure, mate?'

'Sure, you go home. I'll be okay.'

'No, I don't want to leave you, George, give me the gun.'

'You're not taking my gun, limey.'

'George, let me have it and I'll feel happier about leaving you.'

'No, I'll be all right, just let me sleep.'

'All right, George, you sure you will be okay?'

'Yes.'

'How about the wife and kids, are they okay over at my place?'

'Sure, tell them I'm all right, I'm just going to sleep.'

By now it was about 9 pm and I'd been there since 11 am. So I made sure he was in bed and going to sleep and I left. I went home and told his wife that George was fine and was getting some sleep. We had a meal and went to bed. About 2 am I was woken by the sound of crashing glass. I ran into my son's room which overlooked the front of the house and I saw the big bastard ambling down my drive. I ran downstairs, but by the time I reached the drive he'd climbed into his Beetle and was gone – leaving my frosted-glass front door with a big hole in it where he'd thrown a brick. We were all up by now of course, and George's wife was worried sick.

'Look, Angie,' I said, 'we'll have to call the police in – he's gone off his rocker; someone could get killed.'

She agreed and we arranged to meet the police outside his flat. When we arrived there were four police, including an inspector. Up to the flat we went and there was the bloody fool tucked up in bed like a baby. One of the cops said to him, 'You've got a gun and you've just smashed Joe's door.'

'I haven't and I didn't, and I've been in bed all the time,' said George.

That riled me and I shouted at him, 'I bloody saw you, don't give me that shit – and his gun is under the pillow.'

The police found the gun and the bullets and all his sleeping tablets. He kept declaring his innocence and I kept calling him a bloody liar. The police called an ambulance. It was good for a laugh watching the men with the stretcher trying to carry dear George down the stairs. He lived on the fourth floor and he nearly fell off a couple of times. The ambulance attendants were just about done in by the time they got him down – all twenty-four stone of him! Off to Balham Hospital the rest of us went, to find George lying on a bed wearing an operation gown. I went to his bedside and he said to me, 'Sorry, Joe, I didn't mean to do anything.'

'Fuck you,' I said, 'I'm finished with you.'

It was the worst thing I could have said. He got off the bed and the doctor and one policeman tried to stop him. He knocked them to the floor and walked out of the hospital. As he went up the road, I couldn't believe what I was seeing or doing. There was the Zebra staggering in the middle of the road, followed by the doctor, two nurses, a horde of police, me, the inspector, an assistant and an ambulance. I said to the doctor, 'Can't you put a needle in him or something, this is ridiculous?' But we kept on walking and by this time we must have been a couple of hundred yards from the hospital. George decided to sit on the small wall of a garden.

'So what are you going to do?' I said to the police.

'You go and talk to him,' the inspector said. 'See if you can get him into the ambulance.'

I went up to George and showed him, in the lapel of my coat, a little souvenir he had given me, an emblem of a cauliflower ear. He grabbed at it and I grabbed his hand. 'Give me my ear,' he said.

'Let go and I will.' So he let go and I took the ear out of my lapel and gave it to him.

'You're no good, you fucking grass,' he said.

'Go fuck yourself,' I said, and walked away.

They eventually got him back into the ambulance and, God knows why, took him back to his flat. 'What the bloody hell are you doing?' I asked the inspector.

'He's okay,' he said.

Back at the flat the Zebra went to bed and the police gave him back his tablets. It was driving me crazy. The man had tried to kill me.

'He's going to be all right,' insisted the inspector, 'he's given me his word he'll stay in bed. You go home.'

So off I went – round to the back of his flat to his car where I let his tyres down. I wasn't daft, even if the police were. It was now about 7 am and I went home to get some sleep. I was woken by a knock on the patched-up door and my wife looked out of the window of the children's room. It was George – with his tyres pumped up. Down I went in my little vest, nothing else. Looking through the spy hole in the door I saw the Zebra leaning on the other side. I reckoned he might be back to normal by now, so I opened the door and asked him in for a cup of tea.

'Get my wife,' he snarled, and when I turned to look at him I saw he was standing in the passage with the starting-handle of a car in his hand. Thank Christ my wife had the presence of mind to phone the police from upstairs. George heard the extension tinkle and realised what had happened.

'You fucking grass,' he yelled, 'get my wife.' And with that he lumbered down the drive. I whipped upstairs, put my trousers on and went after him. I caught up with him at the entrance to my drive. We were leaning on each other, our noses touching.

'You grass,' he said.

'Go fuck yourself, you crazy bastard,' I shouted back; but I was desperately trying to make a plan of campaign, which isn't easy when you have got a twenty-four-stone man leaning on your nose with a starting-handle in his hand. We slagged each other off and all of a sudden the police arrived.

This time it was a different crew, the heavy mob in three cars. George saw them and he dashed into his car. The police came up and asked George what was happening. George said calmly, 'He's got my wife in there.'

'Have you?'

'Sure, you best go and talk to her!'

One of the policemen went indoors and when he came out he said to George, 'Get out of the car.'

'Go fuck yourself, I'm not moving!'

A twenty-four-stone man in a Beetle is not easily removed. But these were different cops and they knew the story and the game. They dragged him out, and the Zebra knocked two of them down. The others moved in and about six of them pinned him to the ground in the street. His arms were levered up behind him and he was face down. One of the police said, 'Get the cuffs.' Big commotion – no cuffs! 'Well, go and get them. We're not moving.' One went to the car to get the cuffs and the dear Zebra went quiet, not surprisingly with all that lot on top of him. They put on the cuffs and shoved him into the Black Maria. Not a word was spoken. I went back inside and said sorry to his wife, but she had been badly frightened and understood. George was taken to Brixton Prison. He was in court the next day and remanded for medical reports. In the end he was told he could leave prison, provided he went home to America. I went and talked to the promoters and they paid for him and his family to go to America – plus his Beetle, and the starting-handle!

George asked to see me before he left, but I didn't bother. I had had enough of the Zebra.

You only get a handful of friends in a lifetime, that's if you are very lucky. Lou Kay was my best friend. He died in my arms on the dance floor at the Beachcomber Club. I've missed him ever since. I know my life would have been very different if he'd lived.

He was a character all on his own, had more front than Brighton, could and would go where angels fear to tread, and often did. I shall never forget one particular night at the Talk of the Town. Of course we had the best table. Lou had taken the head Maitre 'D' to one side and had charmingly smoothed his palm, strong enough to make sure the star of the show – Eartha Kitt – was looking into his eyes, and he into hers. Lou sounds like a young, slim, good-looking feller, doesn't he? He was fat, really fat, middle-aged and a little on the ugly side (sorry, Mum – you know how I loved him). But with such charm, finesse, manners and confidence. The next thing we knew, he had been invited to her dressing room. After the show we all went off with Eartha Kitt to see Danny La Rue. We had such a party that Eartha Kitt and my wife wound up half asleep on the table before we went home. What a man – my mate Lou! Only he could have managed it.

His flat in Queensway, London, was always full of people, especially girls. I think that every show girl in London had been there at one time or another. Every night a party and, if possible, every day as well. Lou had a knack of getting to know something about everybody. Some secret, that is – but as much as I loved him I never let him into any of mine. No matter how many beautiful girls were in the flat, I'd never go with any, and Lou couldn't understand it. One night he even paid a bird to go to bed with me. I knew this and I played along. I went up to bed with her. Lou, as happy as a sandboy, was in one room, me and the girl in another. I waited a while and then left the girl with an apology explaining that, while she was lovely, this wasn't the night. Later, when I'd left the wife, I didn't give a damn and I'd take plenty of birds to Lou's place. I would let him peek in, even put them in his bed afterwards, and he told me, 'Joe, I'm so pleased, I was beginning to think you were queer.' Funny, isn't it? He had begun to think me queer because I never indulged in his place, and my wife believed I was at it all the time!

The night he died was a reunion for him and my wife of the time. They hadn't spoken for three months. We had gone to the bar at the Dorchester and were having a ball. Lou and she were swearing at each other like mad, it was a wonder we were not banned. From there we went to the Beachcomber. We had the best table right by the dance floor. Immediately Lou was up and onto the dance floor. He danced for an hour. He was so light on his feet for such a big man. At last he came and sat down at the table. He leant over to my wife and said, 'Isn't it wonderful to all be pals again?' And with that he dived into the middle of the dance floor – dead! Just how he would have wanted to go. In the middle of the dance floor, top of the bill, with everybody making a fuss.

The ambulance was called and my wife went with him, while I followed in my car. By the time I got to the hospital there was pandemonium. My wife was trying to get into the room they had him in and the nurses were stopping her, of course. She started complaining that one of the ambulance men had smacked her. I was in such shock that I didn't know what I was doing: I just knocked him for six across the room, and quietened her down. Of course, the police were then called in to settle *me* down!

Eventually we were taken to Lou. Maurice, Lou's brother, had arrived by then as had Sid Epton, Lou's other great pal, and we sat with him. We did not leave him until it was time for the funeral.

He'll never be forgotten – especially by me. Keep one or two warm for me, Lou!

14

The Junior Hoover

Of all the many fights I had with the Zebra, the one I recall most vividly is a match at St Albans. We were having a marvellous bout and in the third round I'd got him in a Boston crab – which means that I had him on his stomach and I was astride him, with a leg under each arm, sitting with my bum on the small of his back, while I pulled back his legs with all my might. I was doing my best to break his back but he was a tough customer and would not give in. When the bell went for the end of the round I bent forward to release his legs. As I did so I fell forward on my hands and knees – and couldn't get up.

The Zebra was helped to his corner but no one came for me because nobody knew I was hurt – and I could not move! The crowd started to laugh, thinking I was messing around and having them on. I was in such searing pain that I couldn't even talk, let alone explain what had happened. So when the bell went for the start of the fourth round I was still on my hands and knees. The Zebra came out of his corner and started to stir up the crowd, telling them that I was too scared to get up and fight. Even he didn't know what I was suffering. So the crowd – *my* crowd – turned against me, booing and catcalling me to get up. Fickle lot, the crowd. Never mind the hours of fun and pleasure I'd given them in the past – tonight is tonight and yesterday is yesterday.

Eventually the fight officials realised that something was seriously wrong and came into the ring to help me. They had to lift me out of the ring in the crouching position and carry me back to the dressing room. Even the crowd realised then that I hadn't been faking and they quietened down. An ambulance was called and I was soon on the hospital X-ray table. They told me I'd torn every muscle in the small of my back, and gave me an injection to ease the pain and help me straighten up a bit. They wanted to keep me in but I declined to be their guest any longer (wonderful people though they were) and asked for a supply of painkillers so that I could get home. They said they couldn't give me enough to keep me free of pain for the forty-mile drive. But a wrestler gets used to pain, and I said that if they gave me another injection I reckoned I could make it. They gave me a jab and I crawled into my car, drove as far as a transport café just outside London and was by then in such agony that I had to pack it up. I asked one of the truck drivers to call my wife and she came out and drove me home. I never went back to the hospital. Instead, I was taken every day for a week to the Turkish baths, where I had

Not just a pretty face: I demonstrate my acting skills in *Trog*.

Two scenes from *Trog*: a) I create havoc. b) With Joan Crawford and a young member of the cast.

Right The Dazzler his best – I pose f the punters. *(Arch Handford Ltd.)*

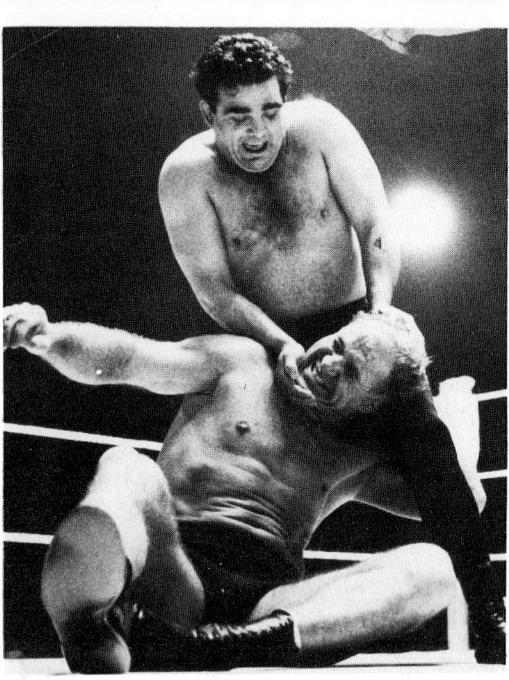

In action with Lucky Sumnavitch, USA. *(H. G. Stevens)*

Right Herman Ifland gives me a tough time in the Royal Show at the Albert Hall. *(Mirrorpic, Daily Mirror)*

With Johnny Peters, my tag partner.

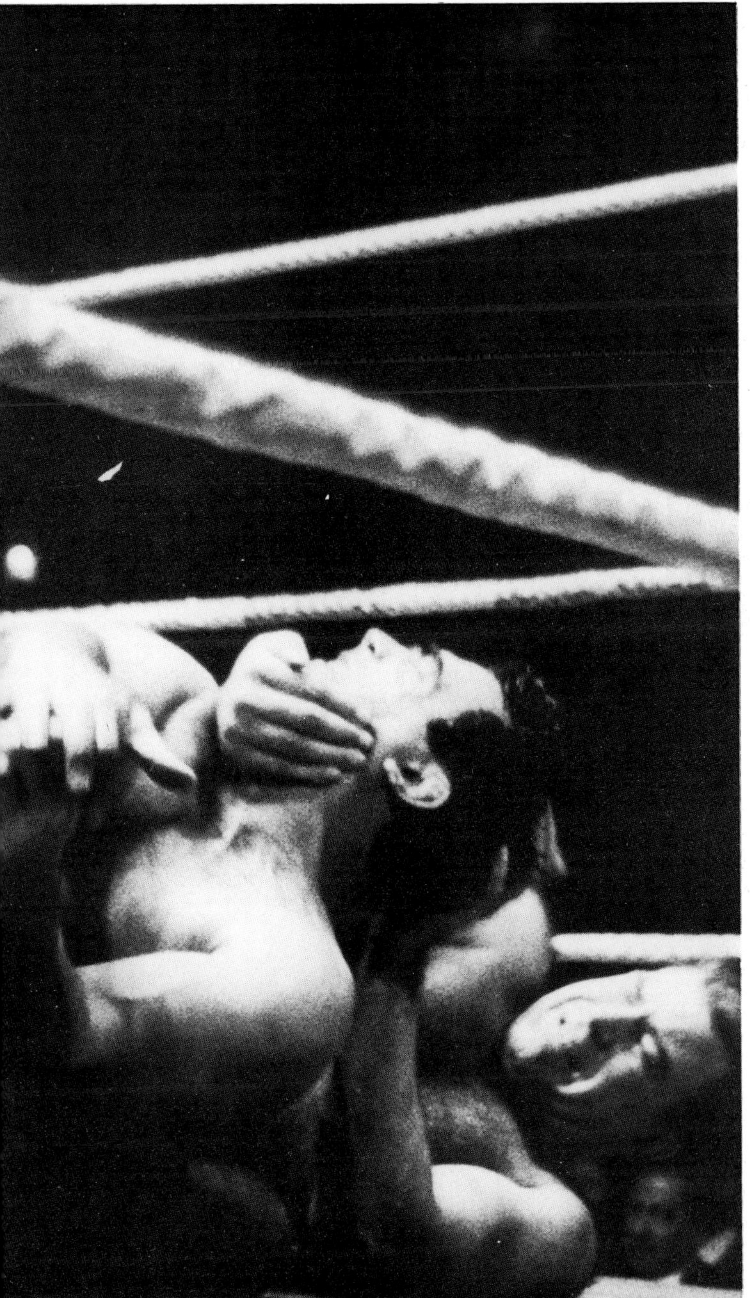

Above A stuntman with style in *Oliver Cromwell.*

Top left In *The Dirty Dozen* with Lee Marvin.

Bottom left Stormy weather ahead. (Left to right) Irish stuntman Frank Haydon, brother Bill, myself and Helmut Griem on choppy seas for a scene in *The Mackenzie Break.*

Overleaf At home with my wife Lindi, daughter Jane, and a small friend.

plenty of heat and lots of schmitzing (rubbing with soap and raffia) and massage. At home I used luma and Epsom salts baths and after a fortnight my back felt great. I've always found that Turkish baths, schmitzing and massage will cure most muscle troubles.

Two more Zebra memories. We were topping the bill at Southampton Town Hall and as I walked to the ring I saw the most beautiful girl sitting in the centre of the hall, about four seats in from the aisle. I thought, what a smasher! I must have a talk with her. The Zebra fought dirty as usual and the crowd got mad at him. So in the third round I contrived to get the Zebra's hand on my face and I screamed and fell out of the ring yelling, 'I'm blinded, I'm blinded.' I staggered and zig-zagged down the aisle, trying to get to the girl. The hardest thing was getting past the sympathetic punters who wanted to help me! I pushed and shoved and twisted, as if I was in pain of course. Half way through the hall, four seats in, I laid my head on her lap. She didn't know what was happening. I cuddled up and told her she was smashing and asked her to come to my dressing room after the fight. Then the customers were onto me and pulling me to the ring to go and kill the Zebra. We put on a fantastic display; but I'm sorry to say the girl didn't turn up after the fight.

Another night at Kingston Baths we had a great bout with the crowds going crazy for the Zebra's blood. When it was over the Zebra went to lie and soak in a bath. There he was, all twenty-four stone of him, locked in a bathroom, safe from me, relaxing as the water lapped over his great big belly, eyes closed, happy. He slowly opened his eyes and there, up in the rafters, he saw me pissing all over him. I nearly fell off the beams watching the poor fellow trying to get out of the bath, slipping and sliding, looking like a whale in distress. I was crying with laughter. I know it's a dirty habit but I just couldn't help it in those days – I'm cured now.

I was always a bit of a joker and showman in and out of the ring but there were times when it didn't pay off – like the night I fought Danny Lynch in Weston-super-Mare. Danny and I were naturals, he being big, blond and ugly, wearing a large leotard to hide his belly, and me being dark, handsome and slim in my beautiful cloak. Our fights always brought great crowd reaction because Danny was such a dirty bastard.

Out we came for the first round – and out of the ring I went. Danny didn't mess about sparring. He aimed me out of the ring straight away and while I was there I kissed a couple of girls in the front row before I climbed back, only – wham – to go out again and kiss a couple of girls on the other side. I went back into the ring and as he went to throw me out again I hit the rope and did my famous head butt, flying across the ring to hit Danny with my head right in his belly. Down he went and I was up and on my way across the ring ready for another flying head butt. As he got up I caught him full in that big stomach again. The crowd were cheering like mad, they wanted me to finish him off. So as he got up again I took him in a side head lock, threw myself up in the air with my body horizontal to him and spun him right over the top of me in a high throw. I asked the crowd, 'Shall I do it again?'

'Yes, yes,' they yelled, so as I got up I grabbed a head lock, jumped up horizontal to him across his body – and he caught me around the thighs and dumped me on the top rope. The rope hit me between the legs, I screamed and he held me there and bounced me a few more times before he elbowed me off the top rope and out of the ring, ten feet down to the floor. The crowd were out for his blood, he was such a dirty fighter.

But Danny just stood in the ring, farting and sticking his fingers up to the crowd. In the meantime a nurse had jumped on me. She must have been sitting on the ringside and she had the sharpest pair of scissors you ever saw. I used to wear a jock strap, a pair of rubber trunks, my tights and then another pair of trunks. But with one swoop of her scissors, this nurse had cut them all away, leaving my poor little sweaty dick and balls hanging out for everybody to see. Then she started massaging my balls and rubbing all around. If she hadn't done it in front of all those people I'd have loved it. But now everyone was watching and I was moaning with delight, though it sounded as if I was in pain. Then to my horror she rounded up half a dozen fellows to lift me right up in the air and carry me through the hall, with all my lot showing. Now when a dick has been sweating it out for hours in a jock strap and has just had a rope whammed up against it, it just shrivels up with fright. Mine wasn't very big at the best of times, but now it looked ridiculous. As they carried me to my dressing room all the wrestling boys were laughing, thinking this would teach me a lesson for playing up so much. I sat on my chair and thought about the crowd and how they'd be saying, 'Poor Joe, what that ugly bastard did to him!' Then as the night wore on perhaps they would be saying, 'Hasn't Joe got a small one?' And they would all start sniggering. Ah well, win some, lose some.

I was the loser again when the boys set it up for me at the Chez Julie night club in Manchester. I'd been fighting on one of the Wryton Promotion shows at Belle Vue and came back with Ronnie Jordan, who did the matchmaking for Arthur Wryton. As was the custom, we went straight to the club. As I came down the steps to the bar and dance floor, there was the most beautiful black girl I'd ever seen. She was with some of the wrestlers, and as I joined them they introduced me and she was on me like a rapist. Her tongue was down my throat, and her hand was down my trousers, trying to get her finger up my arse. I couldn't hold her off – it was lovely, mind you, but she was crowding me like mad. The boys were killing themselves laughing. I held her off long enough to say, 'We'll go to a hotel.' Up the stairs to the door we went and I told her to wait there while I got a cab. But when I got back with the cab she'd gone. Down the stairs I went and the boys were laughing their heads off at lover-boy. I got the needle, but they were so happy I soon forgot about the girl and joined the fun. Mind you, I might have had a lucky escape. A friend of mine (no names) was having oral sex with her, when he climaxed and died. We called her the Junior Hoover.

* * *

Talking about my memories of Zebra reminds me of another great occasion with a very special pal, Johnnie Morgan. Dear Johnnie – the first time we met was years ago at the Caledonian Baths. I'd just been on with Bill McDonald and was in a bath, soothing my poor aching balls – which in itself is yet another story. I was feeling pretty sorry for myself and holding onto my balls which were black and swollen like balloons, when Joe D'Orazio, who had helped me start my career, came in. With him was this blond-haired, good-looking fellow. 'Joe – meet Johnnie Morgan,' said D'Orazio, and explained that Johnnie was a boxer who had boxed pro all over the world and wanted to get into wrestling. D'Orazio wanted to help him get started. Which wasn't any problem, because Joe D'Orazio was my pal and had done so much for me that I felt anything I could do for him would be a pleasure. So, naturally, I agreed.

At that time I had my own small gymnasium in Bermondsey attached to my house, and Morgan used to come down and train with me. Of course he wanted to learn the most complicated moves first, which quite often put me on my head. But it was all great fun and he learnt fast; the important thing was that he was afraid of no one. Which in our game goes a long way in your favour. Johnnie went on to fight some of our best heavyweights and it wasn't long before he was on with Assiratti the Greatest, and they had many blood baths together. But for some reason the promoters would never put the pair of us together. I'd try making requests to work with Johnnie over and over again because I knew we'd have a fantastic bout, as eventually we did. But Johnnie had to promote his own show to do it and he chose to do it in Carmarthen, because he was Welsh. By this time I'd stopped travelling as much as I used to, but when Johnnie asked me to fight I was thrilled, and off I went. Just shows what nuts we are – the very best of pals, but rushing off to knock seven kinds of shit out of each other.

Johnnie picked his old Dad up and then me, and we set off together. We both knew we were in for a great bout and that maybe we both would bleed, but it didn't stop us having a lovely day cruising down to Wales, stopping at different restaurants on the way. What a lovely country Wales is. When we arrived I found to my surprise that no one spoke English. I felt as though I was in some foreign country – as most Welshmen think it is. Good luck to them. Johnnie went off with his Dad and I put up in an hotel. I needed a rest before the fight. The hall, when I arrived, was packed to the rafters. People were standing everywhere, for Johnnie was a great favourite, being so well known from his boxing days.

Fight time comes and I'm sitting in my dressing room – the moment of truth has arrived. Johnnie's my pal; but now it is the time to fight, not love, and I'm very keyed up, the old adrenalin running. It's been a long time since I have seen him fight and I know Johnnie is coming out to show me he is as good as me, if not better, and likewise I have the same feelings. He's my pal, but I'm going to show him who's boss.

We got to the ring and the crowd were going mad, screaming for Johnnie (in Welsh). I thought to myself, 'I'll show these so-and-so's just what a cockney kid can do.' To tell you the truth – I was already getting the needle. You'd think one or two of them would give me a bit of a shout. But no. So I'm thinking, 'I'll show them what I'll do to their Welshman . . .'

We're in our corners, we come to the centre for instruction and I can see by Johnnie's face that he's feeling the same as me and he's going to fight his heart out. 'Right,' I think to myself, 'so be it,' and run back to my corner.

The bell goes and I'm out of the corner like a flash, straight into my famous roll, right into Johnnie's corner, wham, smash – he hits me right in the face with his knee, sending me flying onto my back. 'Blimey,' I think, 'this one has been watching me and learnt fast.' The crowd are yelling like mad. Up I get and as he comes in I roll behind him and get my hands in his crotch, bringing him down flat on his back with me on top. 'How do you like that?' I ask the crowd. The bastards are booing a lovely move like that. I realise that they are totally against me and I'm not going to do anything right. This crowd belongs to Johnnie. 'Well,' I think to myself, 'I'll give them something to boo about.' I pick him up and body-slam him back to the floor, and as he hits it I do a head-spring off his belly. Very nice indeed: it leaves Johnnie clutching his stomach, writhing in pain. The crowd is a bit subdued now. I pull him off the floor, bend his top horizontal to the ground and swing my knee right into his face and I'm loving it. The crowd are really quiet now – their boy doesn't look to be doing too good, and I'm letting them know it. 'I'll give them boo me,' I'm thinking. As Johnnie gets off the floor, I throw him to the ropes and as he comes off I take him over my back and pin him to the floor. First fall to me. The crowd don't like it one bit.

Back in our corners the bell goes for the second round. I do my flying roll, but this time I'm doing it on purpose. As I arrive in Johnnie's corner he throws his knee at me, but I'm ready. I catch his leg and throw it up in the air and over the top rope he goes; out I go after him and give him a whack outside. I've forgotten he's my pal. The crowd had got me at it. They rush at me and get me off while Johnnie climbs back into the ring. While I am still fighting the crowd off, Johnnie is getting his wind back. As I jump back onto the apron of the ring, Johnnie punches me out again and the crowd are going mad – they love him! I get back into the ring, Johnnie body-slams me flat on my back, my wind is knocked right out of me. As I get up – he throws me out of the ring and starts parading around like a champion. I get off the floor and jump onto the apron of the ring and as Johnnie comes to elbow me, I duck, grab his arm and out he comes too. Now we're fighting outside the ring and the crowd are going bananas. I jump back into the ring and run to the opposite ropes, bouncing off them to give me momentum. Now I'm flying through the air to meet Morgan as he climbs back in, with my famous head butt. Down he goes, I grab him off the floor and throw him on to the ropes. As he comes off he drop kicks me – right in the face. Down I go, off to the ropes. He is off at a run across the ring hitting the ropes. Up I get as he is coming at me, I drop to the floor, over me he goes to the next rope. I'm up and off to the opposite one. We are now criss-crossing the ring at 50 mph!

The crowd are standing up shouting for Johnnie.

The ropes around the ring break as Johnnie catches me and throws me against the corner post. As he comes in I throw a punch to his stomach, down he goes and out I go – out of the ring.

Johnnie sees me and starts to chase me. We run round the ring a couple of times and up and down the aisles, he's after me and he is really going potty. I run off – to the dressing room – and Johnnie steams in behind me and slams the door. Outside the crowd are screaming for their man to kill me. We stop and look at each other and catch our breath . . . and sit down, and piss ourselves laughing!

The crowd have had a short, but exciting time and Johnnie and I have had the bout we'd waited for for so long. If it had gone on any longer we might have wound up bad enemies. As it is – we are both sore, but happy.

Johnnie goes out to see his crowd and sign autographs – and I have a pint.

15

Time To Pack Up

I was topping the bill at Crawley in Sussex, when I spotted on the poster, in small print, the name of a man who had been one of my all-time wrestling idols. I won't tell you his name, but he was such a fantastic fighter that when I was new to the game I used to sit in the dressing room praying that he would just say hello, let alone talk to me.

I went to change for my fight, wondering how on earth this great man could have sunk so low. In my dressing room I overheard one of the new boys saying to his friends, 'I'm on with that mug,' and he was talking about my idol. I went up to him and said, 'That man has forgotten more about wrestling than you will ever learn. And if you are ever on with me, take what you can because I'll give you nothing.' It so upset me that I went home that night brooding about how a man can go on fighting when his mind still tells him what moves to make, but his body will not react. It broke my heart to think about it and I vowed it would never happen to me. I made a five-year plan to get out of the game – and stuck to it.

I was able to take the first step because I was a regular at the Russell Square Turkish baths. What a place it was, like a Roman palace – big steam room, hot rooms, ice plunge baths, massage room, lounge and beautiful statues all around you. My friend, Henry Snider, took me there in the first place and it soon became like a drug to me. Every Sunday from about 7 am to 6 pm you would find me there with about twenty-five other regulars. There were millionaires, barrow boys, bookies and wrestlers, and when everybody was undressed you didn't know who had the millions and who had nothing. It was there that I was first introduced to a 'schmitz'. You lie down in the steam room beside a big bucket of soap and a large raffia brush. You then get your friends to soap your body, whirl the raffia over it, then lay the raffia on the body and gently rub you with it. If you can find a place that still does schmitzing, I recommend it for perfect relaxation.

We all used to take food, booze and fruit with us to the baths and about half way through the day we'd lay it all out and have a Roman orgy, without the girls. We would eat and drink, sleep, and go back to the steam. It was a great life. My wife used to complain, but I told her, 'You can moan, groan, leave, do whatever you like, but I'm going down to Russell Square every Sunday.' It was not only the fun, the steam, the massage and the great bunch of fellows that drew me there. I also knew that any aches and pains I had acquired during the previous week's wrestling would soon disappear after a good schmitz.

One day a gay boy came to the baths and we staged a mock trial with him as the accused. My pal, the great Lou Kay, was the prosecuting counsel and Hungarian Sam acted for the defence. The gay boy was in his glory. We sat him on a high chair and crowded round him as Lou was saying, 'I say you came down here with the full intention of sucking a cock or getting fucked. Is that true? Remember you're on oath.' Hungarian Sam jumped up and said, 'I object. It's all supposition. He might have tried to hold a cock, but that's all.' And of course we found him not guilty.

But once we had a gay boy in the steam, and one of the chaps had to give him a back hand for trying his luck too hard. The police were called and there was this constable, helmet and all, in the steam room, trying to find out who did what to whom. Of course, he didn't, but we did offer him a schmitz for his trouble!

Going to the baths changed my way of life. I became a Mason and instead of drinking in pubs on my nights out, I'd go to a dinner and dance. I saw a side to life that I hadn't seen before and I liked it. There was more charity handed out in those baths on a Sunday than lots of concerns ever manage in a year. Henry and I opened a ladies' and kiddies' wear shop, next to my hairdressing shop. Heime was good enough to give me a number of fur hats to sell. I went to another friend, Paul Quadrent, who made skirts.

I said, 'Paul, can I have two of this size, two of that size and two of the other size?'

'You want to sell skirts?' said Paul – and he gave me

about three hundred and fifty of them. 'Now you can sell skirts,' he said. 'Pay when you sell.'

After a while I told Heime I couldn't sell the hats because they were too high class for my shop. 'Then give them to some old ladies,' he said. Such generosity all the time from all the boys at the baths.

Henry was a Jew, so I started to go to the Synagogue with him. I was shocked at first to find everyone talking and waving to each other. I couldn't get over it. I didn't know a Synagogue was a meeting place as well as a place of worship. I joined in with great enthusiasm – I even fasted during Yom Kippur! If I'd wanted to change my religion I would have happily become a Jew. It's more than religion, it's a great race of people. Shalom Malakim.

From that small start with Paul's skirts I was able to work my way out of the wrestling ring. Within a few years I had two very successful ladies' hairdressing salons, as well as a ladies' and kiddies' wear shop in Stockwell and a house in Streatham.

When I learned that the Russell Square baths were going to close I turned the flat above the hairdressers' into a clinic. I installed two beautiful steam boxes and two electric devices – one a faradic machine which worked on the motor nerve of the muscle, making it contract so that you had a work-out while you relaxed. The other was an autoslim which sucked the flesh into a plastic cup, creating a cavity under the skin and allowing the blood to help break up fatty tissues. I also had vibrating beds and vibrating belts, and it was a great little set-up which became very popular. Of course I massaged more girls than fellows, but I gave them the best – and the straightest massage they'd ever had! Every night I was massaging lovely girls. Some of them brought food and booze and gurgled their way through the treatment. When I'd finished massaging they didn't want to go so I used to leave them behind to lock up for me. And when Russell Square did close, all the boys made it to my place for the Sunday orgies. We massaged each other, poured gin into each other in the steam boxes and ate so much we never lost weight. I loved it, and spent far too many hours there – much to my wife's disapproval – so it had to go, and I closed it down.

By this time I reckoned I knew as much about anatomy and physiology as most doctors and I decided I'd like to become an osteopath. So off I went to an institute in Victoria where osteopaths were trained, and applied to join. They asked me what levels of education I had. Of course, I didn't have any and they turned me down. I was choked. I'd spent so much of my life studying anatomy and physiology in gymnasiums, development centres and convalescent centres that I knew the body inside out and backwards. The Army had thought I was educated enough to mend bodies, so why couldn't I do the same in Civvy Street? Why do school grades always matter so much?

I was dwelling on that one morning when the phone went and Billy Robinson, one of the greatest wrestlers of all time, was on the line. He was calling from Tokyo where he was training the Japanese. 'Joe, I want you out here.'

'I'd love to come, Billy, but I haven't wrestled for about a year.'

'It doesn't matter, you never were any good. Get your arse out here.'

I was thrilled, especially when I learned that my old pal Mike Mareno was coming too. We had a great reunion with Billy in Tokyo – until he started telling us about the kind of wrestling we were in for.

'I don't want you messing about with these Japanese,' he said. 'Just go in the ring and fight them.'

'Turn it up, Billy, I'm here for a holiday, not a fight.'

'Okay, have it your way, but these are tough men and they don't mess about.'

'That's fine, I'll make them look good.'

'Don't worry about making them look good, they'll do that themselves. I'm telling you, you'll really have to fight.'

Looking back on it, I think that if I'd known then what I know now, I would never have made that trip. Little did I know what I was in for.

16

Hard Time

They weren't just big, those Japanese. They were giants. And they could wrestle. They were the heaviest, toughest wrestlers I'd ever met – no talking, no showmanship, no communication and no get-togethers. The only time you saw your opponent was in the ring and then he couldn't lose face. They wrestled with everything they had and they knocked seven kinds of shit out of me.

What a state I was in. I hadn't wrestled for a year and I wasn't used to being picked up and slammed down, but they never stopped picking me up and slamming me down because I was letting them do it. I was hoping they would get the message and ease up and let me do a bit of my showmanship. But they never did, they just kept hammering me. They trained for an hour before they went into the ring, while we just warmed up for ten minutes. Their favourite attack was to hit out with a karate blow to my sternum. It was like a big knife being thrust deep in my chest and torn down. I suffered so much pain. I said to Billy, 'You've got to talk to them, they're killing me. I'm here for a holiday.'

'Joe,' he said, 'I warned you, you've got to whack these boys, they don't understand our business. You've got to go back to the cobbles.'

Into the ring I went again that night, out came my opponent and, wham, into the sternum it went again. I was on the floor thinking there was no way I was going to survive this treatment. I just couldn't take another of these blows. They were killing me. The Japanese were quite blasé with me now, thinking they could do just what they liked. They had no respect for me because they'd been doing what they liked to me for a week. I resolved to put a stop to it. As I got to my feet, my opponent came at me like a slaughterman having a ball, thinking what a great man he was to do this to an Englishman. But to hit me with a karate blow to the sternum, he had to step to one side and bring his hand back to do the beastly thing. As he did so I punched him right between the eyes, and as he went down I dived on him, bit his nose, tore his ear, kicked him in the bollocks and never stopped kicking him. The bell was clanging and the referee and cornermen were all trying to get me off. But I was wild and still kicking. I wasn't going to let this bastard or anyone else hurt me again. I was back on the streets and God help them.

For the next four nights I came out of my corner, kick, bollock and bite, and I never left them alone until they were finished. After that it was a different story. 'Ah, Cornelius,' they'd say as they came to the centre of the ring, recognising that it wasn't the same Englishman who was coming out of his corner. Never mind about showmanship, if they wanted a fight they'd get a fight. At last I'd got the message Billy had given me in the first place.

When I packed up wrestling in England I also stopped travelling – unless I could do it in great comfort. But now the Japs wanted to shunt me from one end of the island to the other. Admittedly they had a beautiful coach, quite unlike the cattle trucks the English wrestlers had to travel in at home. But I hadn't gone all that way to start slapping around the roads again. So I told the promoters I had no intention of going all those miles by coach, they'd have to fly me. Mike stood firm with me and eventually we got our way. Mike and I flew everywhere, while the rest of the boys were riding miles and miles in the coach. *Now* it was more like a holiday.

In one of the towns we visited, the arena was in a circular building and the dressing rooms were three storeys up. I was wrestling one of the promoters who weighed 125 kilos. By now, of course, we had sized each other up. I was giving him nothing and he was giving me nothing. Every time he threw me I rolled to my feet. If he body-slammed me I bounced to my feet. I was fit again and beginning to enjoy myself. My joints had got used to the knocks. Sweat was flowing and I was feeling good. I just couldn't resist the sudden temptation. I went behind the Jap and took him to the canvas and goosed him. Thumb up his arse. We had a fantastic match. When it was over and I was back in the changing room, there came a knock on the window. Three storeys up in a circular building and someone was knocking on the window! I opened it and there was my opponent. In he came, bowed low in front of me saying, 'Cornelius very good.' Then out of the window he went and hugged the wall as he made his way along a small ledge round to his dressing room! We couldn't believe it. Billy said, 'Joe, that's never happened before, he must have gone mad.'

A couple of days later at another show, one of the Japanese sent me a message that he wanted to talk to me. It turned out he had lost face with the promoter and needed to impress him. I said, 'Fine, let's talk.' Now in most countries, talking is the easiest thing to do, but not in Japan where the wrestlers were not supposed to communicate with foreigners. Believe it or not, we had to meet in a kids' lavatory where two big wrestlers could only just squeeze in. I made the Jap understand that as soon as the bell sounded he was to run across and throw me out of the ring – and keep throwing me out. The ring was the normal height, but I'd forgotten that, Japanese style, there were no chairs for the punters, who sat around the ring on the floor. So when, according to plan, I went out of the ring at my normal speed with the extra impetus from my giant of an opponent, I caused mayhem in the crowd. I went as far back as possible, arms and legs flaying the air, knocking hell out of those poor punters. And each time I got back in the ring I was thrown out again. All around the ring there were bloody noses and spread-eagled bodies, and on my way back I trampled all over them. In the end I could hardly breathe and had to ask my opponent not to throw me out any more. Not that he understood! Of course he won and the crowd considered him that night's champion. He sent me a message later to thank me for putting him back in favour with the promoter.

Being so fit again I was hungry for sex but Billy had warned me that Japanese girls were different. If you wanted one and you were getting the eye, you didn't do all that courting stuff, you just took her. They reckoned that was manly. There was a little chambermaid who used to come and clean my hotel room, kimono and all, and I noticed she was always giving me sly glances. I tried to be the gentleman but it wasn't getting me anywhere. So I grabbed her one morning and made love – well, it wasn't my kind of lovemaking, it was a straightforward fuck. After that, at eight o'clock every morning, this girl used to come to my room. I'd show her the position I wanted her in, she'd go into it and I'd mount. Eventually I got fed up with this cold-blooded sex and tried to kiss and cuddle her. But it was no good, she just wanted me to show her the position and get on with it. I didn't tell the other English boys about her because they weren't getting any and they might have tried to spoil it for me. I waited until the last day and then took them a loaded French letter (we all used them in those days) and told them to share it out!

Great place for sex, the East. On my way home I bought a few things that caused me some embarrassment at the customs. Funny how they always seem to know when you've got something special in your baggage. They took me behind the scenes, stripped me and searched everything. This was in the days before Britain had any sex shops and I had bought almost every sex aid I could find. There were dildos with funny faces, goats' eyelashes, cream to bring it up, cream to keep it up, vibrators of all kinds, and a form of potato peeling which was banned in Japan. I tried wrapping it round my dick, eating it and all manner of things but I couldn't get it to do anything for me. And I didn't think much of the goat's eyelash which sticks out of the end of your dick and is supposed to stimulate. I had a horrible problem the first time I used it. I had put on the cream to keep the cock up and after I had come I tried to take the eyelash off while I was still hard. I made my cock bleed trying to get it off. I should have waited for it to go down, although with the amount of cream I'd put on to keep it up, it might have stayed that way for ever.

The customs people were very fair and only charged me a minimal amount. They kept a lump of gold I had with me, but I was able to buy it back later.

Driving away from the airport, my car stalled in a blizzard. I couldn't re-start it, but was so glad to be back in England I didn't care about being stuck in the snow. Then from nowhere, a chap pulled up and asked if I was in trouble. He wound up taking me all the way home to Streatham. There are not many of his sort about, and he made my return home perfect.

17

Over The Top

I hadn't been home long before my brother Bill, who was doing very well as a film stuntman, was asked to take a crew out to Ireland. It seemed that the Irish stunt team were fantastic horsemen but not so good in some of the fight sequences which were being shot for a film called *The Mackenzie Break* – later shown on BBC 1. It starred Helmut Griem as a U-boat commander determined to escape from a Scottish prisoner-of-war camp. Bill persuaded me to join his crew of six and off we went, expecting trouble from the Irishmen we were replacing and ready for a fight with them. But we need not have worried, for the Irish boys were perfect gentlemen. We never got to know too much about the plot of the film. We simply concentrated on our stunts, one of which involved abseiling – tying ourselves with a rope to a stake and jumping down the side of a cliff in about four leaps. We started practising on a small tree which suited me fine because of my fear of heights. But brother Bill soon changed all that.

'This is useless,' he said. 'We've got to go higher.'

I tried to talk him out of it but he was adamant.

'If you can do it from twelve feet up you can do it from a thousand feet,' he said, and went off to find the tallest tree in the area. Ten ladders were tied to the side of that tree and climbing up them was a stunt all by itself, never mind the drop! Once at the top you had to tie off onto a main rope that was already hanging there. Then you had to step into space, hoping that everything would hold, and let the rope go through your hands and drop for about twenty feet before you stopped yourself for the first time. Bill led the way and didn't look too happy about it. But he made it and I, his big brother, *had* to follow. When I got to the top, the boys on the ground were just little dots and I was really scared because it reminded me of the 'death drop' I had done in the Army. I prayed to God the rope would hold, stepped off the ladder and let the rope go through my hands until I thought I'd done twenty feet. I stopped – and realised it wasn't so bad after all. I did my four drops and came to earth. After about twenty practice descents I was quite enjoying myself, except for having to climb those ten ladders so many times. Now it was time for Bill to find a cliff at Waterford (where they make that lovely glass) because this scene had to be shot the very next day.

'Choose a nice, gentle slope will you Bill?' I pleaded.

But he took no notice and when we arrived at Waterford we found the ropes were hanging from the top of what, to me, was a ruddy great mountain. 'Right,' said Bill, 'we'll have a practice before we go to the hotel.' (Nice bastard.) Going over the top of a cliff is not the same as stepping off a tree because you have to stand on the edge with your back to the sea and lever yourself over until you are horizontal to the ground before you start your drop. But I did it so often and became so blasé about it that I used to take off my trousers halfway down and show my bum to the boys. That always raised a laugh.

When we had finished the jumping, Bill and I had to do some fight sequences. In one of them we were performing on the roofs of twenty-foot-high Nissen huts, and were swept off by powerful jets from hose-pipes. As soon as the water hit me I had to somersault off the roof and land on special practice boxes which broke my fall. The director liked the shot so much that he asked me to do it without the practice boxes. Instead, the other boys were to run in and catch me before I hit the ground. I said I would do it provided brother Bill was there to save me. So up I went and somersaulted off and there was Bill who caught me under the arms, the silly sod, and let my arse hit the concrete path with a terrible thud. It would have been worse if another member of the crew, Chris Webb, hadn't run in at the same time as Bill and nearly got knocked out by my feet as he broke my fall. As it was, I was paralysed for a moment, but when I stood up I was okay. Don't ask me why, I suppose it was because I was so used to taking bumps. The others had been so worried about me that when they saw me on my feet again they showed their relief with roars of laughter – the whore sons!

* * *

One of the final shots had to be done at sea, quite a long way from our hotel in Dublin. A car was ordered to pick us up at 6 am so that we'd be on the set at 8 am. It was cold that morning so Bill and I decided to warm up by having a drop of poochine with our breakfast – that's the illegal spirit they brew in the hills – it blows your head off. We met up with some more of the boys and had another drop and set off. But on the way we stopped at a beautiful little Irish café cum post-office, cum riding-stable, cum trout-farm, cum anything you can think of. There we had a second breakfast of egg and bacon, sausages, black pudding, potatoes, beans and another drop of poochine. After that, what else could we do but stop at a couple of bars for another drop of the hard stuff. We got to the set about twelve o'clock to find the director going berserk. We had to do only one shot at this location and it had to be finished before the tide turned. It was the scene where Helmut Griem and three other escapers are out to sea, looking for the U-boat to pick them up. We were in a rubber dinghy and Billy and I were rowing when suddenly we saw rocks ahead – and the sea and the wind were driving us on to them. Now Bill and I were rowing like mad and I was shouting, 'Bill, you're doing it wrong, do it this way' (me being a rower).

'Go fuck yourself, I'll row how I like,' said Bill.

'But we're going onto the rocks,' I yelled. 'For God's sake row properly.'

We were both getting het up because it didn't matter how hard we rowed, we were still going onto the rocks. We started to argue and Helmut Griem and Frank Haydon (the top Irish stuntman) were praying that they might be anywhere but in that boat with us, two silly sods who looked like having a fight. Both Bill and I slammed down our oars and sat there, arms folded, defying each other to throw the first punch. And the star said in a thick German accent, 'Please gentlemen, no fighting in the boat.' The rocks were getting closer and closer. The director sent a helicopter to get in between us and the rocks to blow us away from them until a trawler arrived to take us back to the land. By the time we got back the director was so relieved, that he was more than pleased to let us finish the poochine. After that we went back out to sea and finished the shot without further hitch.

In the *File of the Golden Goose*, I was, as usual a heavy and also one of Yul Brynner's gang. I even had a couple of lines to say. You know, I can never get over what fantastic actors these stars are – I'm talking about the others, not me. Though there was one shot in this film where I felt really important.

The gang were on the run, having jumped into this beautiful big Mercedes parked *inside* a garage. The garage doors were locked and the police were all around us. What I had to do was rev the motor and go from the start to 100 mph through the garage doors, down the drive *and* between two big brick-built pillars.

Foot on the accelerator, I revved like mad, the adrenalin pumping, then I took off – WHAM – we hit the garage doors – it was terrific. They flew off their hinges – it was great. The car shot out of that garage so fast that even I was shocked. Then in a split second it all went wrong – one of the garage doors didn't fly away as it was supposed to – it stayed on the bonnet completely blocking my view. There I was – doing what seemed like 90 mph driving towards the two brick pillars – and I couldn't see a thing. 'Shit,' I thought. 'What happens if I hit the pillars. God knows what will happen to us.' And then I thought, 'Fuck it, shit or bust!' I pushed my foot down further on the pedal, tensed my arms and body and hoped for the best. Through the pillars we went – knocking the garage door off the bonnet as we went. I was congratulated by both Yul Brynner and the Director. When I had changed my pants – I felt marvellous. Wish I could really act though.

It was Toni Tensor, the producer, who raised me from film stunts to stardom. Well, I thought it was stardom at the time. Toni called me on the phone and asked me to go and discuss a part he had in mind for me. When we met he looked me over and said, 'Joe, I want you to remember that no one saw Boris Karloff's face in his first film!'

It turned out that the part called for a man in an ape's mask. The film was called *Trog* and when I'd read the script I asked Toni if he was sure I was large enough, because it seemed to me that the script writer was describing a King Kong type of creature. But Toni was happy and I signed a contract for five films if they were needed. It felt like I'd hit the big time.

I was sent off to Charlie Parker, the great artist who did the masks for the *Planet of the Apes*. I had to go to his home every week for months. First he made a skin for my face and then a plaster cast, so that when the mask was finished it fitted every contour of my face. When I put it on I had gadgets in my mouth that controlled the movement of the mask's mouth and tongue. It was absolutely fantastic. Charlie's wife and children had seen the mask in its early stages, but on the morning that it was finished they were out shopping. When they got back and rang the bell, Charlie said, 'Go on Joe, you answer it.' I did – and it frightened them so much, the kids were crying and Charlie's wife went mad and gave him a right rollicking. That mask was a masterpiece. I posed in it for publicity pictures, surrounded by beautiful, half-naked girls, and then I was told that I was to play opposite the one and only Joan Crawford. Wow! This really was the big time. I'd always been a lucky boy – still am – so I thought this was a great omen. For twenty years I'd been a baby-face wrestler. Now I was to be the new villain of the films. Move over, Peter Cushing – here I come!

The film was made mostly at Bray Studios and on the first morning, my chauffeur, if you don't mind, called for me at home in a big black limousine. I arrived to find I had a suite of dressing rooms, a dresser and a make-up girl. When later I met Joan, my cup of joy was overflowing. The director, Freddie Francis, was great to me, always nursing me along. Not that I had anything to say – it was all action. But what a difference it makes being a star, rather than a stuntman. I got so much attention, it made me feel like royalty. And it went to my head sometimes. One lunchtime we were in the restaurant with Bernard Braden and Barbara Kelly's daughter Kim, who was to play Joan's niece in the film. Now Kim had been to stage school and was from a great acting family. She knew all about the game: after all, she had been in it since she was a baby. I don't know what made me do it, but I started getting at her, asking her how anyone so young could possibly know about acting. Being a wrestler, I'd been acting all my life too, so I really knew the game. Kim got so upset she was in tears and called me all the bums she could lay her tongue to – and believe me, she knew a few. She eventually ran out of the restaurant, she was so angry.

The first shot after lunch was of me, strapped to the operating table, after Joan had operated on me to make me speak. Coming to, from the op, I was supposed to look up, see Kim and say 'Ann'. But I couldn't say it – I just burst out laughing at the thought of this big actor who only had to say 'Ann'. I finished up in hysterics and poor Kim was trying to look everywhere but at me because she knew why I was laughing. I was in such a state I had to take my mask off. And every time they tried it again I looked at Kim and doubled up. Delays on a film cost plenty of money, but Freddie was very kind and understanding. He gave us all fifteen minutes to relax and get it together, but even then I had a job to get my one word out. Kim and I had lots of laughs about it later. I never saw much of Joan off the set, she kept herself to herself most of the time. But she was good to me and introduced me to quite a lot of her friends. When the film finished, she sent me a lovely letter thanking me for working with her, and after that I had a card every Christmas. As far as I was concerned she was a great lady and I don't care to read what has been written about her lately.

* * *

Playing the part of an ape made me want to make love like an ape. I invited a pretty starlet to my dressing room for a drink and wound up making love to her in my mask. It just shows what a master mask-maker Charlie Parker was. I could make love with the mask on and didn't know I was wearing it until I wanted a kiss! There's nothing like this method of acting! But try making ape-like love by standing with one leg on the window-sill and the other on the back of an armchair. It's hard work, especially in the short strokes! I'd have done better if they had only put a lady ape in with Guy at the London Zoo. I had spent hours watching him, trying to copy the way he walked and ate before we had started filming.

The film took four months to make, and when it was over that was the end of me as a star because they killed me off and left no opening for a come-back film. But I had no regrets and I'd loved every minute of it. The next week I was a stuntman in *Oliver Cromwell*, and one of the boys said, 'Joe, weren't you a film star last week? What are you doing here?'

I said, 'You can't live on memories, mate, I'm feeding my kids.'

Gerry Crampton, a great stuntman and stunt arranger, asked me to go to Spain on the Oliver Cromwell film. It was to be made on location on a plateau between Pamplona and San Sebastian, which meant that I could save my wages and live on expenses.

There were about six Englishmen who would do the fight scenes and ten fantastic Spanish horsemen for the riding stunts. We lived in a superb hotel just outside Pamplona, and on the first day I was walking up the mountain to the set when in the distance I spotted a shepherd and his sheep. What I couldn't understand was why a Spanish shepherd half way up a mountain should look so familiar to me. As I got within a hundred yards, he turned round, and to my amazement, I recognised Ben Gutura, a Spanish wrestler, with whom I'd had at least a hundred fights. He was a genuine shepherd and these were his sheep, but he was also on the films. What a coincidence! We hugged each other and he told me that most of the horsemen were also wrestlers or ex-wrestlers, and as I had fought most of the Spanish heavyweights it wasn't long before the word whizzed round and they gave me a great welcome. On top of that – I also have Spanish blood.

Mind you, it was the fine horsemanship of the Spanish that stole all the battle scenes. They were proud of their skill and jealous of it. At the start of the film, an English actor came out and swanked about his riding and asked for the best horse they'd got. So they gave him the finest – that is, for stunt work. The poor sod got into the saddle, started to rein back and the horse went up and over just as it had been trained to do. It came back on top of the actor and broke his pelvis. Not very nice, but everyone got the message. The Spanish wanted to keep the riding all to themselves.

During the film, Juan Mahon, one of the greatest horsemen, did me the honour of giving me some riding instruction. I had had a few lessons but I was no expert. He put me on a beautiful big stallion. We were trotting along and he was teaching me to neck rein and turn when all of a sudden my horse took off and we were galloping across the plateau at full tilt with me standing up in the stirrups, loving it but frightened out of my fucking life, and not even trying to pull the horse up. Remember what happened to the actor? I didn't know where the edge of the plateau was but I felt I'd sooner go over it than try to stop. The stallion had got the scent of a herd of mares and suddenly there they were ahead of us. We crashed into them and I thought it was time I jumped off. When Juan arrived I was trying to hold the horse down, because it was rearing all over the place. Juan took him over, gave me his horse to mount and said, 'Joe, I've got to teach this fella a lesson.' He took the horse away from the mares, spurred it into them again, shouted 'Whoa', and then proceeded to knock the life out of the horse, kicking him with the razor-sharp spurs, sawing his mouth with the bit, punching him, and whirling him round and round out of the herd. Then he turned him back and around. Just as he got to the mares again he said, 'Whoa', and that horse stopped dead on his back legs as if he had weights. There was no way he was going to get knocked about like that again. Juan explained that if he had let the stallion get away with it the horse would think it could do what it liked whenever it liked. The Spanish are very strict with their horses, but they love them too. They just know that when cameras are running a stunt horse must do what it has been trained to do on the spot.

Coming back from a battle scene one day, gunsmoke all over me, rotten dirty and tired, I got to the hotel and was just about to enter the lift when an attractive woman stepped into it. By the time we got to her floor we had made a date for dinner. I'd been working on top of a mountain for about a month, windswept, rough and tough, and no women. Was I hungry! When I got to my room I thought I would give her a ring.

'Do you fancy a drink in my room before dinner?'

'Sure, what time?'

'Now, if you like.'

'Right, I'll come down.'

A knock on the door and there she was in a beautiful housecoat, kimono type.

'Come in and have a drink. I'm still hot and dirty – I'll just have a shower.'

In the shower I put plenty of soap all over my body and called from the bathroom for her to come and talk to me.

'My, you are well made!' she said. I had given it a little shine to make sure she saw it at its best. I asked her to do me a favour and wash my back. While she was doing it she told me that she had just sold an employment business and was off on a world trip. Within fifteen minutes we were in bed together and I went down like a champion. It had been so long, it tasted like ice-cream. I love ice-cream and I was eating it all up. She was getting quite excited, rubbing my head and telling me I could make a lot of money doing this. It made me wonder what kind of employment agency she had run. I didn't care: I was having a wonderful time, and went on having a wonderful time for a week. Of course, I had to stop to go to the plateau, but I always came straight back for more. She offered to take me on the trip with her, but I thanked her and told her I was happy on my mountain. You can only eat so much ice-cream.

18

The Contract

The Albion in Pimlico was a pub with a difference – as is Pimlico itself special and different. It was a winner of a pub for me as a publican, and it took a lot of money. Which is just as well because so did my ex wives. It was at the Albion that my so-far charmed life almost came to an abrupt end. Funny really – I'd survived some tense moments in the army, many brutal encounters in the wrestling ring, not to mention my brother Bill's attempt at doing away with me by drowning and flinging me off cliffs – when suddenly one day the telephone rang, and it seemed that my time had come.

I was in the pub office when it rang. I answered and a voice said, 'Is that Mr Cornelius?'

'Yes,' I replied.

'You don't know me – but I've been contracted to shoot you.'

'Fuck off,' I said, never one to be at a loss for words. 'What the hell are you on about?'

'I am going to shoot you, Mr Cornelius.'

I slammed down the telephone. I somehow had the feeling I didn't really want to talk to this chap. However, he made me think – he'd been so very quiet, nice and casual. I've had a few threats levelled at me in my time: the usual 'kick, bollock and bite' – but I'd never had someone tell me in such a gentle, friendly fashion that he was going to shoot me. I tell you – it got to me.

The next day he called again. 'Is that Mr Cornelius?'

'Yes.'

'I expect you recognise my voice – I'm the chap who is going to shoot you – that is will – if you do not agree to do as I ask.'

'What the fuck are you talking about?' I demanded.

'I don't honestly know – all I can tell you is that I have been brought in to kill you if you don't do as you are asked. I'm not to be set loose yet however – I'll let you know when.' And the line went dead.

Now I really started to climb the wall. I just couldn't think of anyone who wanted me dead. In fact at the moment I can't think of anyone who even wants to have a row with me. In desperation I got in touch with a mate of mine who is a bit 'underworld'. He scoffed at the whole idea and assured me no one has any contracts out on anyone.

'You'd better tell that to the cunt on the telephone, because he doesn't seem to know it,' I said.

Another great pal of mine said, 'Stop worrying, I'll come and sit in the bar with you.'

'Oh yes, that'll do some bloody good if he steps in

and starts shooting.' I was really getting worried. I thought about it – after all I'm straight – why not hand it over to the police? Which is what I did.

The police took the matter seriously and arranged to have my telephone line tapped. I honestly had no idea just how difficult it is to catch someone making those kind of telephone calls. And I was losing weight by this time – that's how fucking frightened I was. So frightened, that I had to do something, anything, to prove to myself that I was not a coward. And so I got myself a gun and practised shooting in the cellar of the pub, and when I felt I could really handle it, I went walking. In spite of the fact that I hate the dark, I went walking alone and late at night in all the dark alleys, little streets and old bomb sites. And all the time I was walking, I was nearly shitting myself with fear, but telling myself over and over again, 'Shoot, you bastard, and don't miss.' It is amazing what fear will do. When I think about it now I was so keyed up, I could have easily shot someone, and that really frightens me.

Anyway, the man finally telephoned again and somehow we agreed to a time when he would call me from the call box of the launderette opposite. My mind was spinning with all sorts of possibilities, but my main thought was – he intends to shoot me on the way to or from the launderette. After all there is only a glass partition and glass door to the call box. The time we arranged was 8 pm.

Picture the scene. The tension is unbearable, my brothers are with me in the pub and we are getting more and more wound up. Brother Peter has this big Gurkha knife in the waistband of his trousers and nearly cuts off his cock when it suddenly slips through. Just before 8 o'clock a stranger walks into the pub and looks straight at me. He walked up to the bar, had a scotch and walked out. I told my brother Bill to watch him and see what he does and where he goes. Bill lets me know that he has crossed to the launderette, out I go and zig-zag across the road – anyone could tell I was Army trained and had watched all the best TV shows. I crash into the launderette and run at the man – smash him up against one of the machines, rub him down and spin him around and then rub him down again to see if he has a gun.

'Who?' he whispers, 'what – what's happening?'

'Shut up,' I shout, and throw him away from me and get behind a column looking in at the telephone. Then a tiny chap on a moped stops outside the launderette and comes in. He has a small case. In an instant I am standing over him and he is crouching on the floor.

'Open the fucking thing,' I yell.

'What?' he stammers, all innocent.

'You heard me – open the fucking thing.' I'm mad now, real mad.

The look on my face frightens him and he opens the case. I dive at it and throw out his clothes, pants, socks and vests all over the place. The little chap looks like he is shitting himself. All he is, is a bloke trying to do his washing.

Meanwhile the Rochester Row Police Station are having telephone calls about a madman accosting people in the launderette. I've gone back to the pub. The police come round, I confess, and we all have a bloody good drink!

* * *

I didn't hear from him for over a week. We'd all begun to think it was over and that it was just someone larking about with us. I'd been putting my car over at my brother Bill's. The police dropped in one day and suggested I hide it – just in case the so-called killer 'got' at it. I went out to move it. It was the biggest break we could have had. He called again and my wife answered (she recognised his voice, having listened in with me) and told him I was out but would be back in twenty minutes. She then called the police and only then – me. By the time I got back they had everything set up. Police, GPO tap, and me. I was to keep the bastard on the line for as long as possible.

Suddenly he rang. I try to be casual and I start talking. I have to keep him on the line and I tell him my life story. Suddenly a voice cuts in.

'Joe' (it's Eddie, a policeman I know).

'Yes?'

'It's okay – we've got him.'

'Smashin' – hold the bastard – I'll be round.'

'It's okay – we've got him. You stay there and we'll ring you.'

I tell you we were jumping up and down we were so excited and relieved. It was a wonderful feeling to be rid of that threat hanging over me – I really did think he was going to shoot me.

Eventually I found out what it was all about. Though I could hardly believe it when I did. It turned out to be Norman – the milkman. A right nutter. He was subsequently done on three counts of blackmail, and he had been caught in a telephone box near Dolphin Square round the back of the pub.

You know, when you think you are going to be killed it certainly makes you think. During that period in my life I thought a great deal and came to the conclusion that I wasn't really very nice at all. My main concern was getting on and making a living and making everybody happy – everybody except my own family. I was on stage all the time and I realised what a stupid life I was leading. But I had to suffer a bit more yet before I would accept what was happening to me, and meet Lindi – and really begin to develop as a person.

The first Christmas without my kids did it. It was the worst, the loneliest and most heartbreaking experience I have ever been through. The wife had left me, taking the girls with her, and my son George was off on his own. I took the girls their presents on Christmas Eve and went back to the pub and proceeded to get rotten drunk. No one knew how I felt because when it came down to it no one was close to me. For a man with a million acquaintances, I've only had a handful of true friends. I was suddenly terrifyingly alone. I know that I'd spent years on the road, wrestling, doing film and stage work and I know I hadn't spent all that much time with my children, but I always loved them and showed it. Whatever went wrong between my wives and me – I truly loved my kids.

Christmas morning was hell – no toys, no laughter, no kisses and cuddles – no kids! It was like the wrestling ring – a very lonely place, but this time with no one there to fight. No purpose at all.

I worked hard that Christmas in the pub and spent a while feeling almost happy, having a bottle of champagne with Dad and my brothers. But when they went home, I felt worse. The staff left and I was alone. One minute I had been surrounded by people and now there was no one. Just a big, empty, lonely pub.

I began drinking in real earnest. Pam and a couple of other special friends rang and invited me round to their flat and I went. But there they were – a happy family with their kids and toys and all so good together – I couldn't take it and broke down and left. I went back to the pub, and then had the idea of seeing Toni Mancelli and his wife Lilli. I knocked on their door and they pulled me in. But once more it all got to be too much and I broke and ran. I sat in my car and wondered where I could go, and then remembered a lovely lady who lived in Dolphin Square. I went there and rang the bell. She was as pleased to see me as I was to see her. We had a few more drinks and she asked me to go with her to a party. I remember going, but I was almost in a trance by then with drink and grief. When we got there and had another drink, I was like a zombie. I just sat, not moving, not speaking, just sitting, feeling terrible. I don't remember any more about what happened. All I know is I never want to feel like that again.

19

Lindi

Looking back I have to say that on the whole it's been a great life. I've come a long way from that little cockney kid who spent his Mum's change on pie and mash for his mates and ended up getting his first wrestling lesson from her.

I've fought over three thousand fights – though there were some that seemed like three thousand all on their own. I've made it in my own way on the stage and as a stuntman in films. I've travelled and I've lived. I've made some lifelong friends and some pretty serious enemies too, but after all that's life.

It's been a full and exciting life, and I wouldn't alter any of it – the public side that is, the Joe the crowds knew and loved. But the domestic side has not been a success. In fact, until I met my Lindi, I suppose it would be fair to call it a fucking disaster. ALL my wives left me. . . . They couldn't all be wrong. And yet even with all the problems, the divorces, the heartache, the crippling inroads into my bank account, I DO have something that is very precious to me – my kids. And I still love married life. I'll make sure this marriage works, because I know that this time it's really love.

It's so hard to describe how I feel. You see, Lindi took me on when I was frankly bloody impossible. I'd had so much pain from marriages going wrong, and being without my children, that I was really not at all nice to know. I was spoilt, had too much money, I was bitter and demanding. If things didn't go my way – then they didn't go at all. I have tried walking out on Lindi – well, walk out isn't the word, it was more like a volcano erupting. But Lindi would run after me and tell me to relax, to take it easy, nothing was wrong. And I would look at this lovely woman and see her and think, 'She doesn't have to run after anyone – let alone me.' But she did. She was always there to calm me when I boiled over. I often ask her now, 'Why did you stand for me?' She just stands there and smiles and says, 'I always loved you from the minute I first saw you and I knew there was potential there.' Saucy cow!

I believe at last that I have learnt the real meaning of love and because I have found everything I need in one woman, I no longer need the challenge of other women. I feel happy and content just watching her when she doesn't know that I'm watching her. I know what I want at last, exactly what I want – and I have it. Lindi is my one true love and it is impossible for there to be anyone else for me.

* * *

My love for Lindi is only equalled by my love for my kids. Never has a man been blessed with such a fantastic family. Considering all the upsets in their lives I have caused. Each one is an individual, yet as one. They know they belong to each other and most of all to me. I'm their old man and they know how much I love and respect them.

My Dax is nine years old. He's a great son, short and big-built. He loves sport, loves a fight and has a temper like a tornado. Sounds like my son, doesn't he? And he is as loving as Valentino. His mind is so peaceful and calm, that it is difficult to explain. He is a lovely boy with a lovely mind, a deeply caring child who can get hurt so easily. He is a beautiful, wonderful kid and I am very proud of him.

Jane is sixteen and a beauty with the biggest dark eyes you have ever seen. Wow, what a bird! At the moment she's into boyfriends and dancing and the like. I think she too is very like me, but thankfully she thinks one man is enough. I suppose she came to that way of thinking after seeing her Dad make a mess of things. She's a shrewd girl and like Kay is very reluctant to let people know just how forward she is. One day she asked me for a portfolio. You know, I didn't even know she drew. When I saw her work it was a revelation to me. Oriental in style, so fine, delicate and beautiful. She has a great sense of beauty, though perhaps that doesn't yet show in her style of dress or the way she keeps her room. Jane's at Art School learning design and fashion. I know that one day my Jane is going to be a very big person (though physically she is so small and fine boned!). She is quite a challenge to me and keeps me young thinking about her. We are good friends, Jane and I.

My lovely Kay is such a different scene. I spent a lot of time with her when she was small. As I couldn't take her to the gym and weight training we had long walks together. She did well at school and spent a year in Germany at the age of seventeen with friends of mine. She learnt the language so well that a friend of mine, Peter, says she has no English accent at all in that tongue. Kay doesn't make much of her talents, and is quiet and unassuming. She was always a reserved kid; or at least she was until she went to Sussex University and surprised me by becoming Captain of the Rugby Team with the loudest voice on the field. She is now happily married to her Jim and is a successful business lady teaching aerobics. It's great for me to have a kid carrying our name on in the athletic world. I'm proud of Kay, lovely lady.

George is my eldest. Before he was born I had his room done out like a gymnasium, with weights painted blue, Indian clubs and chest expanders hanging on the walls. The poor little sod had no chance. I'd planned every step of his life before he was even born. By the time he was seven I had him training with me regularly. He was Junior Catch-As-Catch-Can champion and could throw remarkable somersaults. At seventeen he was London Southern Area runner-up to the National Champion. He got a bad decision in the Nationals and said, 'Dad – I don't want to wrestle,' and he became a croupier instead. He was incredibly good at it, one of the five best crap pealers in the world, but he packed it in to come into the pub business with me. Now he's off again making a successful career in International Communications. A great boy and a great man and, most of all, a wonderful son.

These days I am a happy man. I gave up my two pubs in London and found a little pub in the country. I'd had enough of London and the chaps! So here I am, at the Five Bells in Chailey, with my Lindi, five dogs, my kids and the lovely Sussex countryside. I can truthfully say I am as happy as a sandboy.

Telling my life story this way – the good, the bad and the indifferent – has been a strange and very moving experience. It's all told and now I feel it is all behind me. I feel almost reborn, as if I had been given a chance to start life all over again. Only this time I'll be pure and unpolluted – the way my Mum always wanted me to be.